Greece & Rome
NEW SURVEYS IN THE CLASSICS No. 22

GREEK ART

BY
BRIAN A. SPARKES

AF864406

Published for the Classical Association
OXFORD UNIVERSITY PRESS
1991

Oxford University Press, Walton Street, Oxford OX2 6DP
Oxford New York Toronto
Delhi Bombay Calcutta Madras Karachi
Petaling Jaya Singapore Hong Kong Tokyo
Nairobi Dar es Salaam Cape Town
Melbourne Auckland
and associated companies in
Berlin Ibadan

ISSN 0017–3835
ISBN 019–922071–9

© *Oxford University Press, 1991*

Printed in Great Britain
by Bell and Bain Ltd,
Glasgow, Scotland

PREFACE

This survey concentrates for the most part on Greek sculpture and vase-painting of the sixth, fifth and fourth centuries, as it is those subjects and centuries that are most intensively studied in civilization courses. The publications cited are mainly in English, but for a subject such as art, where the illustrations are as important as the text, references to publications in foreign books and journals are inevitable. I have emphasized work done in the last ten to fifteen years but have not denied myself reference to earlier works where necessary. What is included can only be a selection of the material that I should have noted.

I hope that the abbreviations will prove easy to decode; a list of the rarer breeds is appended.

I wish to thank all the museums and scholars who have helped in providing the photographs and drawings with which to illustrate this survey, and all those who have readily given permission for them to be included. The final selection is inevitably something of a compromise; not all that I would have liked to use were available.

Finally, my gratitude to Ian McAuslan for his editorial expertise and to Richard Wallace, the Classical Association treasurer, for his generosity in granting the finance for the lavish illustrations.

CONTENTS

ABBREVIATIONS

I list here the abbreviations I have adopted for works commonly mentioned in the text; I do not list journal abbreviations.

AKGP I and II	*Archaische und Klassische Griechische Plastik*, ed. H. Kyrieleis (Mainz, 1986)
Amasis Painter, Catalogue	D. von Bothmer, *The Amasis Painter and his World, Vase-Painting in Sixth-Century Athens* (Malibu, New York, London, 1985)
Amasis Painter, Papers	*Papers on the Amasis Painter and his World*, ed. M. True (Malibu, 1987)
Amsterdam Symposium	*Ancient Greek and Related Pottery, Proceedings of the International Vase Symposium Amsterdam 1984*, ed. H. A. G. Brijder (Amsterdam, 1984)
AntPl	*Antike Plastik* (Berlin)
Beazley Addenda	L. Burn and R. Glynn, *Beazley Addenda* (Oxford, 1982) and T. H. Carpenter, *Beazley Addenda* (2nd edition, Oxford, 1989)
Beazley and Oxford	*Beazley and Oxford*, ed. D. Kurtz (Oxford University Committee for Archaeology, Monograph no. 10, 1985)
Beazley Lectures	*Greek Vases, Lectures by J. D. Beazley*, ed. D. C. Kurtz (Oxford, 1989)
Blanckenhagen Festschrift	*Studies in Classical Art and Archaeology, A Tribute to Peter Heinrich von Blanckenhagen*, edd. G. Kopcke and M. B. Moore (Locust Valley, 1979)
Boardman *GSAP*	J. Boardman, *Greek Sculpture, the Archaic Period, a handbook* (London, 1978)
Boardman *GSCP*	J. Boardman, *Greek Sculpture, the Classical Period, a handbook* (London, 1985)
Brommer Festschrift	*Festschrift für F. Brommer*, edd. U. Höckmann and A. Krug (Mainz, 1977)
Copenhagen Symposium	*Proceedings of the 3rd Symposium on Ancient Greek and Related Pottery, Copenhagen August 31-September 4, 1987*, edd. J. Christiansen and T. Melander (Copenhagen, 1988)

Eikones	*Eikones, Festschrift Hans Jucker*, edd. R. A. Stucky and I. Jucker (*AK* Beiheft 12, Bern, 1980)
Eye of Greece	*The Eye of Greece, Studies in the Art of Athens*, edd. D. Kurtz and B. Sparkes (Cambridge, 1982)
Greek Vases	*Greek Vases in the J. Paul Getty Museum* I–IV, *Occasional Papers on Antiquities* 1, 3, 2 and 5 (The J. Paul Getty Museum, 1983, 1985, 1986, 1989)
Himmelmann Festschrift	*Festschrift für Nikolaus Himmelmann*, edd. H.-U. Cain, H. Gabelmann and D. Salzmann (Mainz, 1989)
Kanon	*Kanon, Festschrift Ernst Berger*, ed. M. Schmidt (*AK* Beiheft 15, Basel, 1988)
Lausanne Colloque	*Images et Société en Grèce ancienne. L'iconographie comme méthode d'analyse. Actes du colloque international, Lausanne 8–11 février 1984*, ed. C. Bérard, C. Bron and A. Pomari (Lausanne, 1987)
Moon *AGAI*	*Ancient Greek Art and Iconography*, ed. W. G. Moon (Wisconsin, 1983)
Parthenon-Kongress	*Parthenon-Kongress Basel, Referate und Berichte 4. bis 8. April 1982*, ed. E. Berger (Mainz, 1984)
Praestant Interna	*Praestant Interna, Festschrift Ulrich Hausmann*, ed. B. von Freytag gen. Löringhoff, D. Mannsperger and F. P. Wasmuth (Tübingen, 1982)
Robertson *HGA*	M. Robertson, *A History of Greek Art* (Cambridge, 1975)
Robertson *SHGA*	M. Robertson, *A Shorter History of Greek Art* (Cambridge, 1981)
Rouen Colloque	F. Lissarrague and F. Thelamon, *Image et céramique grecque, actes du colloque de Rouen, 25–26 novembre, 1982* (Rouen, 1983)
Tainia	*Tainia, Festschrift für R. Hampe*, edd. H. A. Cahn and E. Simon (Mainz, 1980)

TEXT FIGURES

COLOUR PLATES

I. INTRODUCTION

The rise in popularity of school and university courses in Classical civilization, and the related decline in the study of the Greek and Latin languages, have given Classical art, and above all Greek art, a prominence that it never enjoyed before. Increasingly good photographs, the chance to see architecture and art in its local context that improved travel facilities have brought, the need for the material to be seen in its historical setting, and the necessity of explaining the intricacies of the study to a wider audience, all these have produced a wealth of new publications.

These new works include one-volume histories, of larger or narrower compass, books that concentrate on one medium (sculpture, painted pottery, terracotta figurines, etc), and much more specific volumes that look more closely at a brief period or restricted region, or even an individual building or a single vase-painter.[1] All this is underpinned by a massive output of more academic literature in journals in all languages that gradually alters our knowledge or understanding of the subject.[2] Such changes are brought about by new finds (one thinks of the Riace bronzes (Figs. 8–9), the tomb of Philip II of Macedon (Colour Plate 1B), the Mozia youth (Fig. 5), the kouros from Samos (Fig. 3), the New York Euphronios krater), but new interpretations are also brought about by a fresh look at old material and ideas, a move down different avenues with new preoccupations and emphases. Recently there has been greater stress on the contexts within which the craftsmen of ancient Greece worked and for which they made their products. Pure aesthetics are seen as too inward-looking an approach, Greek art and craftsmanship did not exist in a hermetically sealed vacuum; the social, historical, and religious background to any work of art is felt to deserve an important share of the scholar's and the student's concern. Also, the need to judge the significance of material that has survived against the whole production of any period has been urged, and the 'positivist' approach (i.e. an emphasis on or a restriction to considering only that which has survived) has come in for some hard knocks.

Conferences and museum exhibitions are two ways of disseminating new ideas, and the *Acta* and *Catalogues* that stem from them are useful publications of up-to-date ideas and finds (here one thinks of the Parthenon Congress at Basel, the Amasis Painter Exhibition in New York and elsewhere, the Athens Conference on Archaic and Classical sculpture).[3] Other museum publications attempt to present the material in a manner that is intelligible to the student and the casual visitor alike, a difficult task at which the British Museum has recently shown a marked ability.[4] Full-scale catalogues are now rarely produced by the larger museums,[5] but some private owners have their own more modest collections published (e.g. Bastis, Hunt, Ninagawa).[6] However, in recent years, the legal and moral aspects of collecting and retaining antiquities have come under close scrutiny.[7]

Greek Sculpture

Sculpture is central to any study of Greek art, and here more than anywhere we must be conscious of what survives and what has been lost.[8] We are at the mercy of historical accidents, and what we have is for the most part an unrepresentative selection of what was produced, heavily biased towards stone sculpture and, within that reduced orbit, in favour of sculpture as architectural decoration. The quality of the best work cannot be denied and can be appreciated for itself, but we are still haunted by the ghosts of lost masterpieces, whether in bronze or marble, or gold and ivory. The Riace bronzes (Figs. 8–9) have for many (though not for all) pulled aside a veil or two (see pp. 15–17); the recently restored and displayed fragments of life-size gold and ivory figures (Colour Plate 1A), found beneath the Sacred Way at Delphi in 1939, go a little way to help in reconstructing the appearance of Pheidias' chryselephantine colossi of the mid fifth century B.C., and show that the technique was being practised at least a century earlier.[9]

Scholars still look closely at copies and at literary references for new insights, as indeed is necessary, even though the study of copying has recently been dubbed 'perhaps the oddest phenomenon in all Classical scholarship'.[10] Certainly copies are now less trusted to give a precise reflection of an original, they are seen more as adaptations that need to be viewed within the context of their own period of manufacture and of the social milieu that valued them, and for what they say of the taste of the owners who paraded them.[11] Such works look odd in 'modern' books amongst original Greek sculptures, but the very juxtaposition of copies and original works has its own pedagogical effect. The late and fragmentary written sources are also now viewed with a more guarded eye; but Pausanias, Pliny the Elder, Lucian etc., continue to yield assistance.[12] Equally, in more general terms, historians, orators and such provide vitally useful social and economic information on the background to the craftsman's world, and inscriptions add their weight to the total picture.

New approaches, however, are taking an increasing part. As instances one might mention the scientific study of different marbles and other materials, the composition of bronze and the techniques of the manufacture of large scale statues, the logistics of transporting stone, especially in the early period, the outdoor setting of Greek freestanding sculpture in sanctuaries, cemeteries, etc., the nature of colouring on stone (both as a background to sculpture and on masonry), Greek sculpture and Roman taste, the impact of Greek works in Rome.[13] Though style still absorbs the attention of scholars, it is increasingly stressed that it is not autonomous, it cannot be divorced from subject matter, and both must be seen in relation to purpose – was it a public or private commission? who was responsible for the choice of subject? what relation does the imagery have to military or political events, or to social structures? This in turn has sharpened the need to establish the chronology of Greek art in relation to historical events.

The Siphnian Treasury at Delphi – a case study

With all this in mind, let us as a preliminary consider one of the monuments as a case study – the Siphnian Treasury at Delphi (Fig. 1).

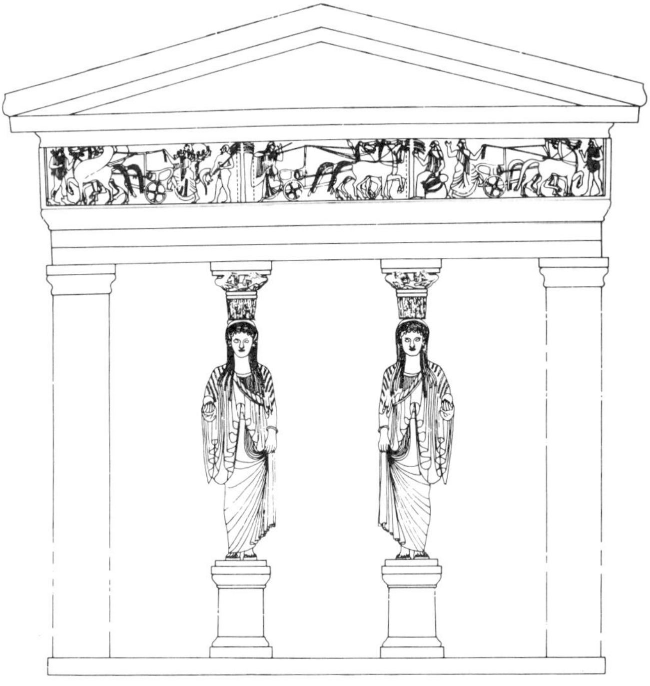

1. Siphnian Treasury, Delphi. Ca. 530 B.C.

It has come in for some close investigation recently. The building in question stood at the far west end of the first leg of the Sacred Way at Delphi, turning its back on the pilgrims as they approached from below. Only the foundations mark the spot; the decorative sculpture now enhances the museum (Fig. 2). The friezes have for long been

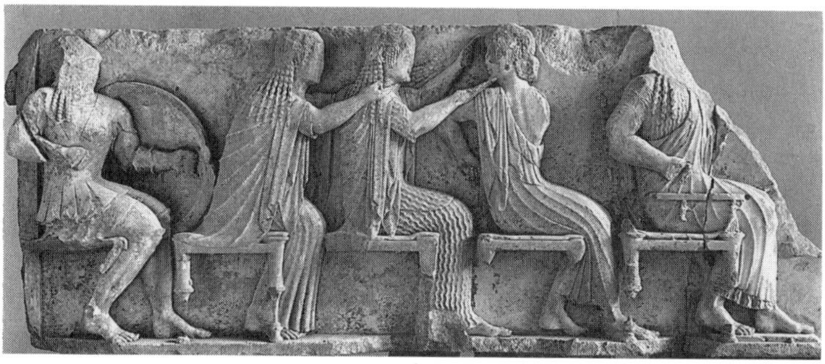

2. Detail of East frieze of Siphnian Treasury, Delphi. Ca. 530 B.C.

considered jewels in the crown of Late Archaic art. The architectural decoration was given its 'official' publication back in 1928;[14] much more recently the building itself has been exhaustively published in the same series.[15] But there is still room for disagreement, and the various approaches and discussions encapsulate some of the interests, difficulties, and attractions of the study of Greek art.

On the basis of recent publications, new interpretations, and new findings, we might express the approaches as questions:

1. Are we right in connecting the ruins and the sculptures that are associated with them, with Pausanias' (10.11.2) and Herodotos' (3.57–8) Siphnian Treasury? Doubts have once more been thrown on the identity of the two,[16] and although these doubts do not detract from the quality and interest of the friezes, dissociation will naturally put them in a different context. More seriously, if we are not dealing with the Siphnian Treasury when we study the friezes, then we are cast adrift from what has always been considered one of the more firmly fixed dating points in Late Archaic art.

2. But how secure is the date of the Siphnian Treasury, even if we are to suppose that the building and its sculptures have been correctly identified? Herodotos (3.57–8), in the course of his narrative of the Persian king Kambyses' invasion of Egypt (525/524 B.C.), makes a complicated connection between Samian pirates, Polykrates, and Siphnos. Traditional understanding of the connection places the

collapse of Siphnian wealth at that time, and thus the erection of the treasury at Delphi in the years immediately preceding the raid on Siphnos by Samian pirates in 525 B.C. Thus the date is usually given as ca. 530 B.C. If it is possible, as has been suggested,[17] to disengage the completion of the building from that decade 530–520 B.C. and suggest a different, later chronology for some of the events, then our whole understanding of Late Archaic architectural sculpture is flawed. This has repercussions for our dating of Attic vase-painting, as the closest comparanda with the Siphnian figures are to be found in the work of the Andokides Painter in very early Attic red-figure.[18] There has been reluctance to follow the new dating, but the fact that the problem can be raised is of interest.

3. What are the subjects of the friezes and how were they arranged? One subject has never been in doubt – the North frieze that faces the Sacred Way shows the battle of the gods and giants. Comparison with Attic black-figure vase-paintings has enabled Mary Moore to present us with a more detailed picture of the frieze as a whole,[19] and a strong light on the lettering has sharpened some of the readings and altered others.[20] Almost all the gods' names are now certain, and there is a more logical connection in the flow of the narrative. The same scientific work on the lettering has made the East frieze more intelligible. The two juxtaposed scenes were always seen to be connected with the Trojan War: a discussion on Olympus (Fig. 2), and a duel on the Trojan plain. The new readings help to suggest a different connection between the two halves from that previously supposed. The battle is between Akhilles and Memnon over the body of Antilokhos whom Memnon has killed (an episode related in the *Aethiopis* of Arktinos), and the scene in heaven shows the weighing of the destinies of the fighters, the balance held by Hermes, in the presence of their mothers, Thetis and Dawn, a theme well known in vase-painting.[21] Mary Moore has also given us a clearer idea of the West front of the treasury (Fig. 1), where the tripartite division of the frieze matches the architectural setting in which it is placed, above antae and caryatids.[22] Here the subject is the Judgement of Paris, with the three goddesses distributed in the three sections, the chariots ready to leave, and Paris, his task completed, somewhat marginalized above a column. The South frieze is still desperately fragmentary, and although the old interpretation of the scene as Kastor and Pollux carrying off the daughters of Leukippos is still considered the likeliest subject, there is much space to fill.

4. But why were these particular subjects chosen? Are they to be considered a unity? Or are they random choices from the deep well of mythology? And what of the pediments? Also, what of the caryatid

korai in the porch and the Victories as akroteria on the roof? Do they all hang together as a programmatic plan devised by the priesthood at Delphi? Some ingenious attempts have been made to inject political significance into the stories, seeing them as warnings against hybris with specific reference to the tyrant of Athens and his allies.[23] Certainly, the battle of the gods and giants is an unusual choice outside of Athens where it has special significance in relation to the robe of Athena. The Struggle for the Tripod in the East pediment has been seen as an allusion to the 1st Sacred War[24] and also once more to Peisistratos and Athens. Downdating of the building to a time after the Persian Wars has been thought to give significance to the Victories and the caryatids, and to provide an anti-Persian context for the whole programme.[25] As can be seen, there is no shortage of contenders for a political significance.

5. Who carved the friezes? This question may be tackled on a general and a personal level. Two 'masters' have usually been distinguished, master A of the West and South and master B of the North and East, a distinction based on style but also suggested by the 'signature' on the North frieze: '[. . .] made these and those behind'. The style of each is clear: A's flat technique and sensitive rendering of horses (the korai are thought by some to be his); B's more active, robust figures (he may have carved the East pediment). A is usually thought to have been an Easterner, an Ionian most likely, as is shown by the winged Athena and the high crowned heads, whereas B has Athenian affinities but has also been claimed for the Cyclades. On a specific level, the 'signature' on the North frieze fails to clarify the issue, especially as it is fragmentary and difficult to read – we may have 'Endoios of Attica', 'Daippos', 'Aristion of Paros'.[26]

As can be seen, the Siphnian Treasury continues to raise all manner of questions; and questions of the same sort continue to be addressed to other monuments and statues.

Painted Pottery

The sheer numbers of painted vases that have been preserved make them an inevitable subject for study, whether for archaeological, economic, or aesthetic reasons. The quality of many of them, and the subject matter of the scenes depicted, make them suitable material for art-historical treatment.

General books on Greek pottery continue to be needed. Robert Cook's *Greek Painted Pottery* is still a basic tool for the whole field, with Dyfri Williams' more recent and slighter *Greek Vases* a useful and attractive introduction.[27] The balance in some works is different. Ingeborg Scheibler's *Griechische Töpferkunst* casts the net wider, looking at shapes, techniques, and trading, with less emphasis on individual painters and connoisseurship.[28] Indeed, although interest in connoisseurship is still strong, there has been some realignment of interest, with more concern with shapes, functions, trade, and the status of the craftsmen in the potters' shops; in the study of figured scenes, interpretation, purpose, and meaning have also been considered afresh. Again, as with sculpture, there has been stress placed on the need to see pottery against the culture within which it was made.

A Note on Chronology

There has recently been a lively exchange of views about chronology, particularly that of the Late Archaic period. Battle has raged on all fronts, with the chief protagonists of change being Michael Vickers and the late David Francis: Geometric pottery on Near Eastern sites, the destruction levels observed on the Athenian Acropolis and in other parts of Athens, Archaic coinage, the dating of 'kalos' names on Attic pottery, Herodotos and buildings, ostraka, the political significance of Theseus, the Aphaia temple on Aegina, etc. What has been exposed is a tendency to circularity of argument amongst the traditionalists and the shakiness of some of the foundations of what had been thought to be 'fixed' absolute dates. Robert Cook's recent itemized summary[29] of the arguments for downdating, and his own comments on each item, make detailed treatment unnecessary here. He finds the revised chronology 'much less credible than the conventional one' but warns that 'the conventional chronology is much less sure than is often supposed'. The traditional chronology is retained here, but there are valid criticisms of the system that have still not been answered. The interlocking of the different sets of evidence is by no means a perfect fit.

NOTES

1. Of general books, G. M. A. Richter's *Handbook of Greek Art* (9th edition, London, 1987) is still useful for the illustrations but is looking old-fashioned (it first appeared in 1959). M. Robertson's *A History of Greek Art* (Cambridge, 1975) and *A Shorter History of Greek Art* (Cambridge, 1981) are richer in both content and depth. J. Boardman's *Greek* Art (3rd edition, London, 1986) still provides a good short introduction, and D. Haynes' *Greek Art and the Idea of Freedom* (London, 1981) and S. Woodford's *An Introduction to Greek Art* (London, 1986) are both lively. More detailed works are mentioned in the notes.

Mention might be made here of the Plate Volumes to the new edition of the *Cambridge Ancient History* vols. III– (Cambridge, 1984–); they have detailed descriptions to the illustrations. A single volume for the whole of Greek art, organized on the same lines, is planned. Gratitude is also owed to the Greek publishers Ekdotike Athenon S.A. for their transformation of Greek archaeological publishing; material from Greek sites and museums is at last available in splendid colour photographs.

2. Keeping track of new evidence and new publications is a never-ending task. Besides *L'Année Philologique*, help is available in *Archaeological Reports* (issued annually with *The Journal of Hellenic Studies*); 'Chroniques des Fouilles' which is a section of *Bulletin de Correspondence Hellénique*; *Fasti Archaeologici*; and for ceramics, H. Metzger's biennial resumé of recent publications in *Revue des Études Grecques* is an invaluable aid.

3. *Parthenon-Kongress Basel, Referate und Berichte 4. bis 8. April 1982*, ed. E. Berger (Mainz, 1984); D. von Bothmer, *The Amasis Painter and his World, Vase Painting in Sixth-Century B.C. Athens* (Malibu, New York, London, 1985); *Archaische und Klassische Griechische Plastik*, ed. H. Kyrieleis (Mainz, 1986).

4. E.g. B. F. Cook *The Elgin Marbles* (London, 1984); D. Williams, *Greek Vases* (London, 1985).

5. As exceptions one might instance the volumes published by the Museo Nazionale Romano, I. *Le sculture* (1979–); II. *Le pitture* (1982–); III. *Le terrecotte* (1983–); IV. *I Bronzi* (1983–); V. *Le ceramiche* (1986–); and B. Vierneisel-Schlörb, *Glyptothek München Katalog der Skulpturen* Band II. *Klassische Skulpturen des 5. und 4. Jahrhunderts v. Chr.* (Munich, 1979) and Band III. *Klassische Grabdenkmäler und Votivreliefs* (Munich, 1988).

6. *Antiquities from the Collection of Christos G. Bastis*, ed. E. S. Hall (New York, 1987); *The Wealth of the Ancient World, The Nelson Bunker Hunt and William Herbert Hunt Collections*, ed. J. K. Tompkins (Fort Worth, 1983); Erika Simon, *The Kurashiki Ninagawa Museum* (Mainz, 1982).

7. See K. E. Meyer, *The Plundered Past, the traffic in art treasures*, rev. ed. (Harmondsworth, 1977); J. Greenfield, *The Return of Cultural Treasures* (Cambridge, 1989); *Archaeological Heritage Management in the modern world*, ed. H. Cleere (London, 1989). See also III n. 11.

8. R. Lullies and M. Hirmer's *Greek Sculpture* (2nd edition, London, 1960; now in its 3rd German edition, 1979) is still a helpful start. J. Barron's *An Introduction to Greek Sculpture* (London, 1981) is an enlarged version of his *Greek Sculpture* of 1965. W. Fuchs, *Die Skulptur der Griechen* (2nd edition, Munich, 1979) is a useful handbook, organized by types; for a useful work of reference, see W. Fuchs and J. Floren, *Die griechische Plastik* I, *Die geometrische und archaische Plastik* (Handbuch der Archäologie, Munich, 1987). A. Stewart, *Greek Sculpture: an exploration* (Yale, 1990) is a magnificent pair of volumes. B. Ashmole's *Architect and Sculptor in Ancient Greece* (London and New York, 1972) is a classic study of architectural sculpture. King's College London now houses the Ashmole archive of photographs.

9. Boardman *GSAP* fig. 127. See P. Amandry, 'Chios and Delphi', *Chios, a conference at the Homereion in Chios 1984*, edd. J. Boardman and C. E. Vaphopoulou-Richardson (Oxford, 1986), pp. 205–32, esp. 228–32; C. C. Mattusch, *Greek Bronze Statuary, from the beginnings through the fifth century B.C.* (Cornell, 1988), pp. 176–81. For the silver bull (dedicated by Croesus?), see P. Amandry 'Statue de taureau en argent', *BCH* Supplement 4 (1977), 273–93 and for the à jour ivory reliefs, see J. B. Carter, 'The chests of Periander', *AJA* 93 (1989), 355–78. For the workshop finds for the Pheidian Zeus, see II n. 36.

10. Boardman *GSCP*, 8.

11. M. Bieber, *Ancient Copies, Contributions to the History of Greek and Roman Art* (New York, 1977) represents the traditional approach; B. S. Ridgway, *Roman Copies of Greek Sculpture, the Problem of the Originals* (University of Michigan Press, Ann Arbor, 1984) studies the subject from fresh angles (location, accessibility, etc.). See also P. Zanker, *Klassizistiche Statuen* (Mainz, 1974).

12. J. J. Pollitt's *The Art of Greece 1400–31 B.C.* (Englewood Cliffs, 1965; Cambridge, 1990) gives a good selection of the documentary sources for Greek art, mainly sculpture. On Pausanias, see now C. Habicht, *Pausanias' Guide to Ancient Greece* (University of California Press, 1985).

13. For identification of marbles, see e.g. C. Renfrew and J. S. Peacey, 'Aegean marble: a petrological study', *BSA* 63 (1968), 45–66, pls. 11–13 and B. Ashmole, 'Aegean marble: science and common sense', *BSA* 85 (1970), 1–2. For the composition and techniques of bronze-making, see B. S. Ridgway, 'The Lady from the sea: a Greek bronze in Turkey', *AJA* 71

(1967), 329–34, pls. 97–100; C. C. Mattusch, *Greek Bronze Statuary, from the beginnings through the fifth century B.C.* (Cornell University Press, 1988) with earlier bibliography. For the transport of marble, see A. M. Snodgrass, 'Heavy freight in Archaic Greece', P. Garnsey and others (edd.), *Trade in the Ancient Economy* (London, 1983), pp. 16–26. For the setting, see B. S. Ridgway, 'The setting of Greek sculpture', *Hesperia* 40 (1971), 336–56, and R. Barber, 'The Greeks and their sculpture: interrelationships of function, style and display', *Owls to Athens: Essays on classical subjects presented to Sir Kenneth Dover* (Oxford, 1990), pp. 245–59. On colour, see V. J. Bruno. 'The painted metopes of Lefkadia and the problem of colour in Doric sculptured metopes', *AJA* 85 (1981), 3–11, pls. 1–3 and I. D. Jenkins and A. P. Middleton, 'Paint on the Parthenon sculptures', *BSA* 83 (1988), 183–207. On the impact of Greek art on Rome, see C. C. Vermeule, *Greek Sculpture and Roman Taste* (Ann Arbor, 1977) and J. J. Pollitt, 'The impact of Greek art on Rome', *TAPA* 108 (1978), 155–74.

14. *Fouilles de Delphes* IV.2. *Art archaique: les trésors 'ioniques'*, by Ch. Picard and P. de la Coste Messelière (Paris, 1928), pp. 57–171.

15. *Fouilles de Delphes* II *Topographie et Architecture, le trésor de Siphnos*, by G. Daux and E. Hansen (Paris, 1987).

16. M. Vickers, 'Persepolis, Vitruvius and the Erechtheum Caryatids: the iconography of Medism and servitude', *RA* (1985), 3–28, esp. 9, n. 36. See now in answer, P. Amandry, 'A propos de monuments de Delphes; questions de chronologie (I)', *BCH* 112 (1988), 591–610.

17. E. D. Francis and M. Vickers, 'Signa priscae artis: Eretria and Siphnos', *JHS* 103 (1983), 49–67. See now in answer, J. Boardman, 'Signa tabulae priscae artis', *JHS* 104 (1984), 161–3.

18. D. von Bothmer, 'Andokides the potter and Andokides the painter', *Metr. Mus. Bull.* February 1966, 201–12.

19. M. B. Moore, 'The gigantomachy of the Siphnian Treasury: reconstruction of the three lacunae', *BCH* Supplement 4 (1977), 305–55.

20. V. Brinkmann, 'Die aufgemalten Namensbeischriften an Nord- und Ostfries des Siphnierschatzhauses', *BCH* 109 (1985), 78–130 and see E. Simon, 'Ikonographie und Epigraphik. Zum Bauschmuck des Siphnierschatzhauses in Delphi', *ZPE* 57 (1984), 1–22, pls. 1–7.

21. L. D. Caskey and J. D. Beazley, *Attic Red-figure Vases in the Museum of Fine Arts, Boston* 3 (Oxford, 1963), no. 147.

22. M. B. Moore, 'The west frieze of the Siphnian Treasury', *BCH* 109 (1985), 131–56.

23. L. V. Watrous, 'The sculptural program of the Siphnian Treasury at Delphi', *AJA* 86 (1982), 159–72, pls. 17–21; cf. W. Stern, 'The horsehead-helmet giant on the Siphnian Treasury frieze', *AJA* 87 (1983), 261. See now R. Vasić, 'A note on the theme of the Siphnian frieze', *Boreas* 7 (1984), 34–40. See also K. Arafat, *Classical Zeus* (Oxford, 1990), pp. 147–50.

24. H. W. Parke and J. Boardman, 'The struggle for the tripod and the first Sacred War', *JHS* 77 (1957), 276–92 and J. Boardman, 'Herakles, Peisistratos and sons', *RA* 1972, 57–72. For the tripod scene, see D. von Bothmer, 'The struggle for the tripod', *Brommer Festschrift*, pp. 51–63, pls. 17–19.

25. See n. 16.

26. On the signatures, see A. Rumpf, *Cr. Arte* 3 (1938), 44–48 (Endoios); M. Guarducci, 'Lo scudo iscritto nel fregio del tesoro dei Sifni a Delfi', *Studi in Onore di Luisa Banti*, ed. G. Becatti et al. (Rome, 1965), 167–76 (Daippos); L. H. Jeffery, *Archaic Greece: the City-states c. 700–500 B.C.* (London, 1976), 185 (Aristion).

27. R. M. Cook, *Greek Painted Pottery*, 2nd ed. (London, 1972); D. F. Williams, *Greek Vases* (London, 1985). *A History of Greek Vase Painting*, by P. E. Arias, M. Hirmer and B. B. Shefton (London, 1962) is now out of print; a German version, *Die griechischen Vasen*, by E. Simon and M. & A. Hirmer 2nd ed. (Munich, 1981), has a slightly different selection of photographs. Fascicules of the *Corpus Vasorum Antiquorum* continue to appear; there is now an excellent key to the mysteries of its arrangement and distribution in *Summary Guide to Corpus Vasorum Antiquorum*, compiled by T. H. Carpenter (Oxford, 1984). For the Beazley Archive of photographs and drawings of Greek vases, see p. 42.

28. I. Scheibler, *Griechische Töpferkunst: Herstellung, Handel und Gebrauch der antiken Tongefässe* (Munich, 1983).

29. 'The Francis-Vickers Chronology', *JHS* 109 (1989), 164–70. Some of the particular items are mentioned later.

II. MASTERS, HANDS AND FREESTANDING SCULPTURE

Both in sculpture and in vase-painting, the identity and personality of individual craftsmen still exert a strong attraction. The cult of the creative artist is too deeply ingrained in our own thinking to be jettisoned totally in favour of other, more impersonal considerations, and so there is much scholarship still carried out from the point of view of the individual. The name of the artist may be known to us through the historical tradition as preserved in the literary sources or through the random discovery of names in inscriptions. The absence of a name says nothing about the quality of a work, its presence may tell us much about the posthumous standing of the artist. It is good to be reminded that working with the names of artists that we know, is a very restricting method of proceeding, it is as if we possessed a complete list of sculptors actually at work and had only to pick a name from the list.[1] Connoisseurship has shown that the name may be an unnecessary addition, the very workmanship declares the hand, and with aesthetic sensitivity and stylistic analysis scholars can create lost personalities. Some studies widen the point of view and consider the stylistic elements that go to make up a region, others prefer to think in terms of works, not artists and to consider sculpture as a manifesto that needs to be set against its historical background.

Archaic[2]

Kouroi and korai are the only types of Archaic freestanding sculpture that exist in any numbers, and have been used as the yardstick for the study of Archaic statuary in general. Gisela Richter's large volumes[3] are basic, even though now considered by some as sterile taxonomy. Eleanor Guralnick[4] has extended Richter's patient logging of measurements and through the use of photogrammetry and computer-executed techniques generally, has considered the profiles and proportions in relation to foreign influences and body types of athletes in various sports. However, Anthony Snodgrass's statement that 'the better sculptors came to regard it [the kouros] as a tiresomely inhibiting and convention-bound medium'[5] points to the dangers of the positivist approach.

Meanwhile, study continues. Andrew Stewart[6] has looked at the meaning of the figures in general and sees the statues as 'basically meaningless', 'empty vessels awaiting content, and needing only a label or a context to signify'. He sees them as 'impersonal representations of Man', with their nudity their only attribute, symbolizing the values of the élite with their self-indulgent generosity, and their disappearance is dubbed a Late Archaic reaction to aristocratic rule. He traces their development from generic to individual, a direction that Brunhilde Ridgway would reverse,[7] as she sees korai initially as major goddesses whose meaning is then broadened to include nymphs and lesser deities. Much work is being done on the regional workshops: Mainland, Cyclades, Ionia, North, and West; progress is inevitably slow.[8] Against such criteria as place of discovery, historical conditions, source of marble, dedicatory inscriptions and signatures, and style, one must set the movement of artists and the dissemination of motifs. Thus we have korai made locally in Cyrene by East Greek immigrants and a draped kouros in Syracuse that has links with Ionian workmanship.[9]

In his indefatigable search for inscriptions, Claude Vatin has argued that the Delphi twins were originally marked as Kastor and Polydeukes and that their connection with Herodotos' Kleobis and Biton (1.31) is a pretty fiction.[10] He comforts us with the thought that 'L'émotion provoquée par la disparition de Cléobis et Biton ne doit pas faire oublier tout l'intérêt que présente une image aussi ancienne des Dioscures.' Not all scholars are convinced. A closer look at two other old favourites shows perhaps that too often we accept earlier theories and statements. It is now suggested that we must remove the famous Lyons kore from the list of freestanding korai and give her an architectural function in front of a small naiskos,[11] and a recent detailed study of the Kritios Boy shows him taller than we had been led to believe and the context of his discovery to be even less straightforward than we had feared.[12]

New finds continue to astonish and amaze, for one reason or another. The new Getty kouros has been castigated as a forgery; we must await full publication.[13] The sanctuary of Hera on Samos, which has already provided outstanding archaic material, still continues to give up its fallen and buried treasures. Two striking newcomers are a marble kore and kouros.[14] The kore belongs with the well-known figure in the Louvre dedicated to Hera by Cheramyes – indeed, it is its 'twin' (same epiblema, mantle, and chiton) dedicated by the same man and without doubt carved by the same sculptor. The base of the monument has been found, and there was room for four figures – perhaps another kore and a kouros? The new kouros (Fig. 3) is even more startling. Dedicated by Iskhys (the inscription on the thigh is a later version of what was most likely carved on the original base), the kouros dates from ca. 570 B.C., is three times life size, c. 5 m. tall, and made of local grey-veined marble.[15] Helmut Kyrieleis suggests that we should think of an heroic ancestor, usually

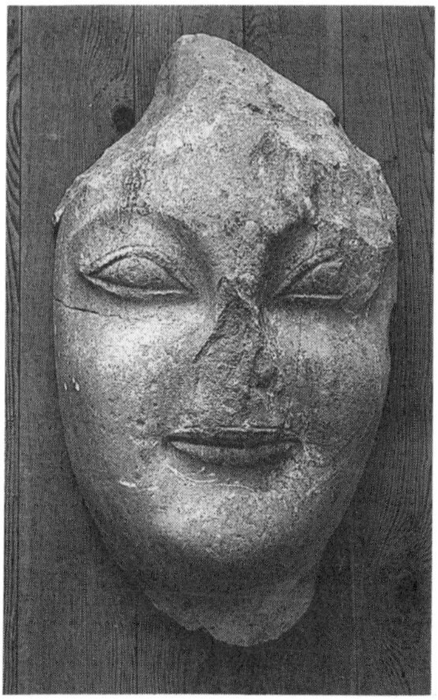
3. Head of Iskhys kouros, Samos. Ca. 580–570 B.C.

considered by the Greeks to be of colossal size. The Iskhys kouros has the advantage over many others of a preserved face and base block. It will now surely serve as a point of reference for any study of local Samian style as well as being seen as a masterpiece of Archaic art in itself.

Some kouroi and korai have been grouped together as the works of one or other unnamed artist; perhaps best known is Payne's linking of the Rampin rider and the Peplos kore as the works of one man.[16] Others start with a known name (whether from inscription or literary source) and attribute various works to the same man. Aristion of Paros, working in Attica in the third quarter of the sixth century, is known from signatures on bases, and the discovery at Merenda in Attica of Phrasikleia herself, whose base had been known since the early 18th century, initiated a search for pieces from the same hand. The funerary kouros of Kroisos, from Anavyssos in Attica, is suggested as one of Aristion's major works,[17] and his influence, if not his hand, is seen in such pieces as the Rayet head and fragments, and the Theseus and Antiope from Eretria. Antenor, of the late sixth century, who is known in literature as the maker of the first bronze group of the Tyrantslayers for the Athenian Agora, also made the majestic Akropolis kore, as the inscription on the base testifies.[18] Other figures that have been linked stylistically with the same sculptor, include some figures (attendant korai and Victory akroteria) on the East pediment of the Apollo temple at Delphi, and the remaining pediment of the Apollo temple at Eretria, which includes the same group that was seen to be influenced by Aristion. Such circularity renders plausible the view that we are dealing with regional, chronological, or social identity, not with personal style.

An interesting exercise in conjuring another name from the shadows and solving a longstanding problem concerns Euthydikos' kore and the Blond boy, considered to belong stylistically together and to look forward to the West pediment of the Zeus temple at Olympia, this last, of course, bafflingly attributed by Pausanias (5.10.8) to Alkamenes of Athens of the later fifth century. To cut the knot, John Barron[19] has suggested that an elder Alkamenes was responsible for all three, as well as for the Hermes before the Gates of the Akropolis which now ceases to be an archaistic statue and becomes a truly archaic piece. Such a career would have spanned the Persian Wars and would help to bridge the divide between Archaic and Classical that our nomenclature falsely perpetuates.

Classical[20]

With the Classical period comes the disparity between the literary testimonia and the anonymous mass of Greek sculpture and Roman copies. Thus any new original material found is likely to be seized on and inserted into the existing framework, to reinforce its structure or to alter its shape. Particularly is this so with the new bronze finds (mainly from the sea), for bronze now takes on a special importance. Proportion of known to unknown is still very small, but the new pieces afford us a clearer picture of the quality of bronze working and have brought into greater prominence, and raised important questions about, the nature of copying and adaptation.[21]

An interesting workshop find has been made at Baiae on the Bay of Naples; it consists of plaster-moulded casts of bronze originals.[22] Full-size casts must have stood in the studio with armatures to hold the plaster-covering in place. So this brings us one step nearer than the 'copies' themselves to the missing originals but at the same time brings to the fore the lack of consistency in the 'copying' process. The drawback with the finds is that they are mainly very fragmentary and only preserve small elements of the statues; the advantage is that enough remains of some pieces for them to be identified with well-known statues: the 'Westmacott boy', the Berlin and other Amazons, the Athena Velletri, the Hera Borghese, the Apollo Belvedere, the Nemesis of Rhamnous (see p. 18), etc. The best known are the fragments of the later Tyrantslayers, especially the face of Aristogeiton (Fig. 4). It has been pointed out that the eyelashes which would have been very delicate in the original bronze statue, have been protected in the mould and would need attention when the marble worker started on the face.

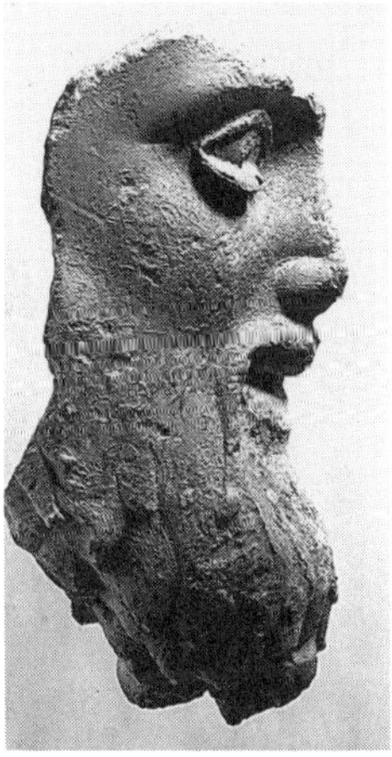

4. Plaster cast of face of Aristogeiton, Baiae. 1st c. A.D. copy of original of ca. 477 B.C.

The reputed date of 477 B.C. for the Tyrantslayers[23] has also been suggested for the Piraeus bronze Apollo. This statue has always fluctuated alarmingly in its dating, from mid sixth century to Late

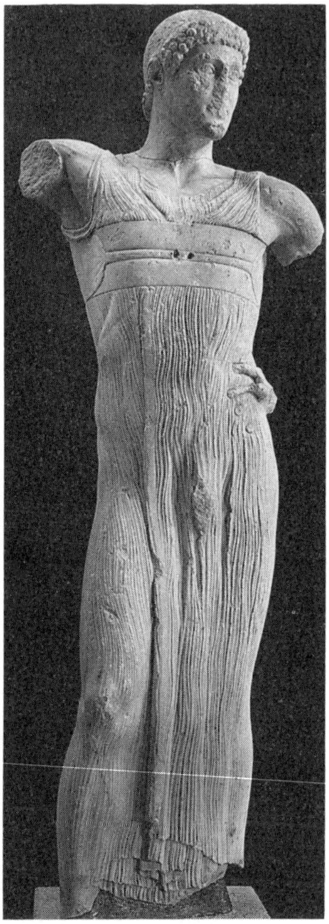

5. 'Giovane de Mozia', from Motya. Ca. 470 B.C.

Hellenistic. George Dontas[24] has now suggested that it is a consciously archaizing piece dating from after 480 B.C. and based on a version of a kouros of the mid sixth century, and he links it, as he does the other statues in the Piraeus find of 1959 (the Athena and the two Artemis figures), with Delos. For the Apollo he has a particular date and occasion, connecting it with 477 B.C. and the foundation of the Delian confederacy. By contrast, the Delphi Charioteer[25] still retains a steady calm not only in appearance but also in its dating in the 470s (478 or 474 B.C.) – a welcome stability. The long robes of the charioteer have been seen again on what many consider to be a contemporary marble statue, from the Carthaginian site of Motya in Western Sicily.[26] The statue (Fig. 5) shows a man dressed in a long, clinging tunic that is curiously held to his body by a very large belt. With the loss of his right arm, it is difficult to understand the meaning of the gesture. He has been interpreted as a charioteer (but why the raised arm?), and in view of the strong Punic connections of Western Sicily he has also been seen as a priest of the Phoenician god Melkart. There is also disagreement over date – 470–450 B.C. or around 400 B.C.? The marble is thought to be local Sicilian (from Selinus?), but the origin of the workmanship is obscure. It is by the discovery of such a piece as this that our vision is widened and the depth of our ignorance all too clearly revealed.

There is now a cluster of bronzes around the middle years of the fifth century. The Zeus (not Poseidon) of Artemision,[27] of ca. 460 B.C., is joined by three others. The bronze fragments found in the waters off Porticello at the toe of Italy, especially the bearded head (Fig. 6) instantly dubbed 'Il Filosofo', have brought to the fore once again the place of portraiture in Greek art.[28] A few scholars would divorce the head from the rest of the wreck, the cargo of which places it around 430 B.C., and make the figure into a Hellenistic philosopher. Certainly the realism is marked. However, the major publication of the fragments and the associated wreck maintains their connection and reviews possible subject matter. The suggestion that what we have are fragments of a group comprising the centaur Chiron and the young Achilles, his pupil, is now abandoned, and 'on strictest evidence, it can only be stated that the Porticello sculptures depicted an elderly and probably mythologico/monstrous creature, at least two young men in athletic nudity, and perhaps a third wearing a short garment' and 'it may even be helpful to repeat that no assurance exists as to the connection of all fragments, which may well belong to independent statues rather than to a single narrative group.' The date suggested for the group is ca. 460 B.C. which places it in the Early Classical period when more realistic detailing of features and anatomy is to be found on the pediments of the Zeus temple at Olympia; also, the centaurs of the Parthenon metopes come within the orbit of that particularization. The Ostia portrait of Themistokles (Fig. 7) still teases[29] – a copy of an original made just before or soon after his death in 462 B.C., or a copy of a very clever pastiche of much later?

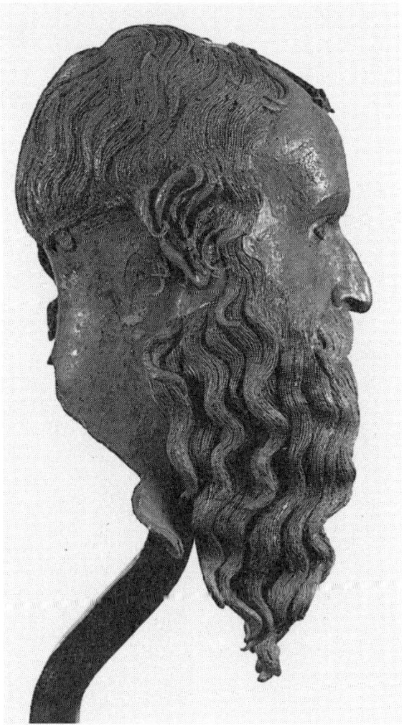

6. Bronze head, from Porticello. Ca. 460 B.C.

The Riace bronzes (Figs. 8–9) have claimed much of the limelight.[30] Scholars have rushed upon them like moths to a flame, and the output of fact and interpretation has been tremendous. After attempts to downdate them to Hellenistic, most scholars would now see them as originals of the mid fifth century. Absence of context leaves open the gate to speculation on all fronts: whom do they represent? what were they holding? do they belong together? when were they made? are they the same date? where were they made? where were they set up? for what occasion? who made them? Answers to all these and similar questions have varied considerably. It has been inevitable perhaps that all the great names of fifth-century Greek sculpture – Kresilas, Myron, Alkamenes, Onatas, etc.[31] – should have been brought into play here, but that Pheidias should be frontrunner, as it were, is indeed remarkable.[32] The association of the pair with the Athenian dedication for Marathon at Delphi, with which literature connects

Pheidias' name, though not without its problems, has proved enormously attractive.

We are always wanting to get closer to Pheidias, to try and understand the essence of his great reputation. The Riace bronzes have been thought to help towards that aim but in so doing have also

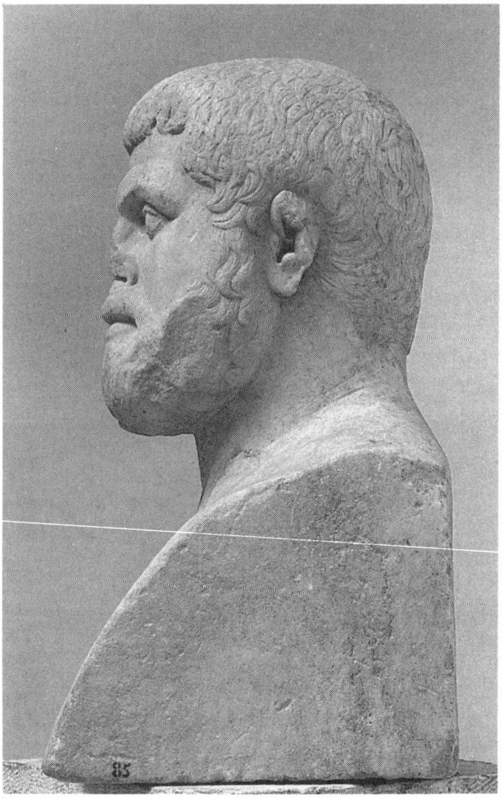

7. Herm of Themistokles, from Ostia. Copy of original of ca. 460 B.C.

affected other aspects of the study of him. The Athena Lemnia on the Athenian Akropolis has figured in most histories of Greek sculpture, conjured up by Furtwängler from a body in Dresden and a head in Bologna. But, though perhaps correctly reconstructed, may she rather represent another Pheidian figure? A theory is gaining ground that the reconstructed figure was the Athena from the Marathon dedication at Delphi,[33] and for the Athena Lemnia Eve Harrison suggests that we should be looking for a different type of figure.[34] Harrison has also pointed out that a head from the Athenian Agora (Fig. 16)

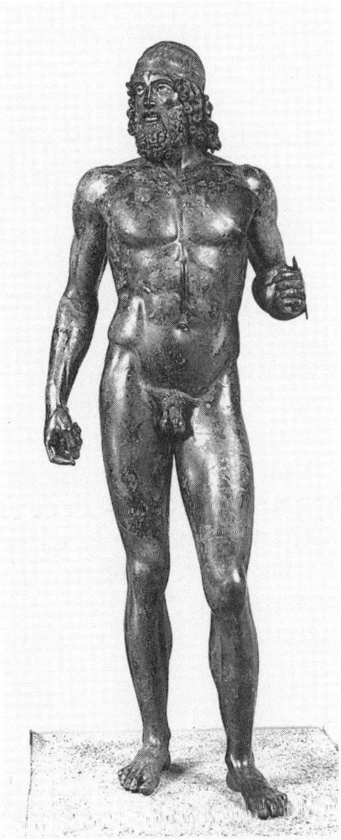

8. Bronze statue A, from Riace.
Ca. 450 B.C.

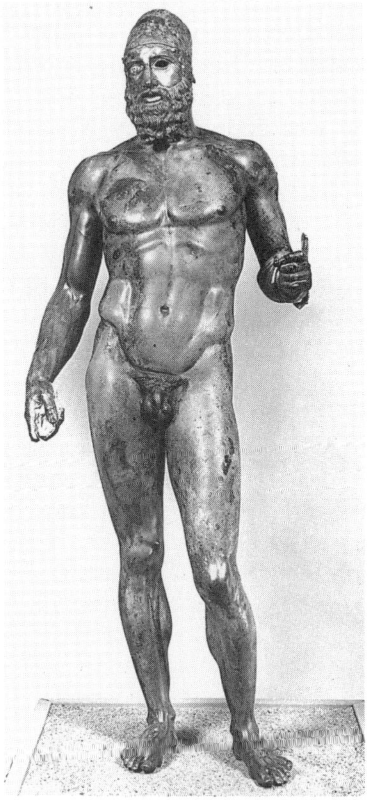

9. Bronze statue B, from Riace.
Ca. 450 B.C.

may be a true-size copy of the Victory on the hand of Athena Parthenos (for the Parthenos and the Parthenon, see pp. 28–33).[35] Pheidias' seated Zeus figure for the temple at Olympia has some of the moulds for the gold preserved, and there now seems to be a late fifth-century Athenian bell-krater that copies the Niobid story from the throne, only a generation after it was set up.[36]

Myron is still a shadowy figure, perhaps not made any clearer by being saddled with the Riace bronzes and certainly not when given the friezes of the Hephaisteion in Athens.[37] Kresilas is best known for his portrait of Perikles (full figure, of course, not merely a head). Pandermalis has set the strategos portraits of the fifth century in order, and Harrison has sorted out Kresilas' place in the chronology of the fifth century.[38] Polykleitos has perhaps provided less attraction, though the Kanon has not ceased to invite theories and the Amazon competition still seems to show no signs of ceasing to provoke polemic.[39] Later in the century we have Alkamenes (now the younger, see pp. 12–13 above), a pupil of Pheidias, who worked until the end of the century. The Prokne and Itys group on the Athenian Akropolis continues to attract attention.[40] Pausanias (1.24.3) tells us that the group was dedicated by Alkamenes, but some have suggested that it was also made by him, whilst one recent theory builds on an earlier idea that the group was occasioned by Sophokles' tragedy on the theme, and sees the dedication as having originally read 'dedicated [by Sophokles and made] by Alkamenes'.[41] His name has also been connected with the caryatids of the Erechtheion and the figures of the Apollo Sosianus temple in Rome.[42]

Eve Harrison has helped us to see Paionios in a clearer light by removing the Hertz head from the list of copies of the Victory figure at Olympia, thus bringing the sculptor firmly into the later part of the century.[43] Agorakritos of Paros is another sculptor who has emerged more clearly from recent work, especially by George Despinis and Basil Petrakos.[44] His best known statue was the cult figure of Nemesis made ca. 430 B.C. for the temple out in the Attic countryside at Rhamnous (Fig. 10). Despinis' patient assembling of fragments from the site has given a notion of the appearance of a late fifth-century

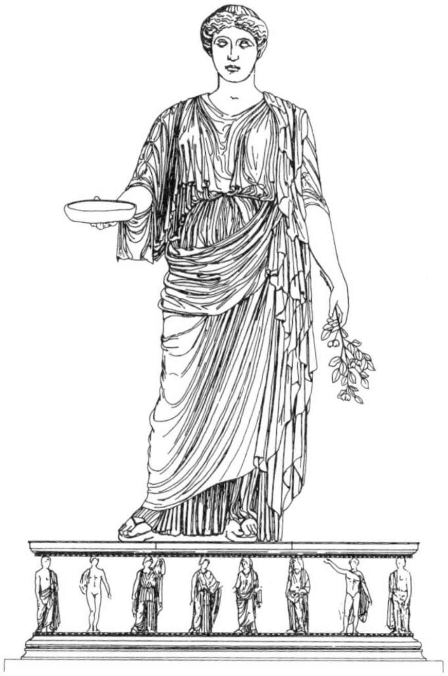

10. Cult statue of Nemesis, Rhamnous. Ca. 430 B.C.

cult statue, whilst Petrakos' work on the fragments of the base has enabled us to envisage the total effect of the composition.

The great names of the fourth century exert as much fascination on scholars as those of the fifth. Kephisodotos' name has been connected with the big bronze Athena from the Piraeus find, and the existence of a marble copy of the bronze has enabled the relationship of the original and copy to be seen in a more complex way than formerly.[45] We must not expect too accurate a facsimile of an original, many are free adaptations of earlier works rather than precise transcriptions. The Hermes and Dionysos group at Olympia has rarely been out of the limelight since its discovery last century, and the precise connection of Praxiteles with it has often been a matter of polemic. The group was found on the spot where Pausanias (5.17.3) had seen it, and the identification of text and statue was for long accepted. There were dissentient voices, and Sheila Adam in 1966[46] considered that technically the carving was too advanced for the mid fourth century. In one of his last articles R. E. Wycherley[47] reviewed the veering fortunes of the group, with useful and revealing quotations from earlier writers. He himself took the traditional view that the statue was an original by Praxiteles and noted that Pausanias never used the word *techne* other than in reference to an actual work. Since that review of the evidence and views, Katharine Morrow[48] has studied the footwear of Greek sculpture and has shown that Hermes' sandals are of a type that is not otherwise known in the fourth century and finds parallels in the second century B.C. The battle continues.

If we have to release the Hermes group at Olympia from the actual hand of Praxiteles, it may be possible to recompense him with another group. The column of the Dancing Maidens (Fig. 11) has been a major attraction in the Delphi museum since its excavation in the 1890s.[49] It is perhaps not to present-day taste with its column topped by massive leaves, the three maidens back to back with kalathoi on their heads and framed all round by a massive tripod. Are they Bacchants, Thyiades, Cecropidae or what? The whole structure stood 11 m high, and perhaps at ground level in the Delphi Museum proximity tells against it. In a recent study of the eastern side of the base of the momument[50] Claude Vatin claims to have revealed two inscriptions, one below the other. One reads:

> '. . . when Leokhares was archon at Delphi
> . . . when Hippodamos was archon at Athens [375–374 B.C.]
> having taken (spoils) from the Spartans to Apollo
> Pythios, the Athenians and their allies
> dedicated the tripod and the maidens.'

and below it 'Praxiteles made'. There is also another inscription:

'. . . . .
Timotheos dedicated to the Pythian
making a new alliance of Victory
and the People of the Athenians.'

So the monument was erected by the Athenians and their allies with the Second Athenian League, for their victory over the Spartans at Alazeia in Akarnania in 375 B.C., with Timotheos, son of Konon, who commanded the allied fleet, taking charge of the dedication. So, if the readings are correct, we have an (unsuspected) original work of the young Praxiteles and a date fixed for its erection.

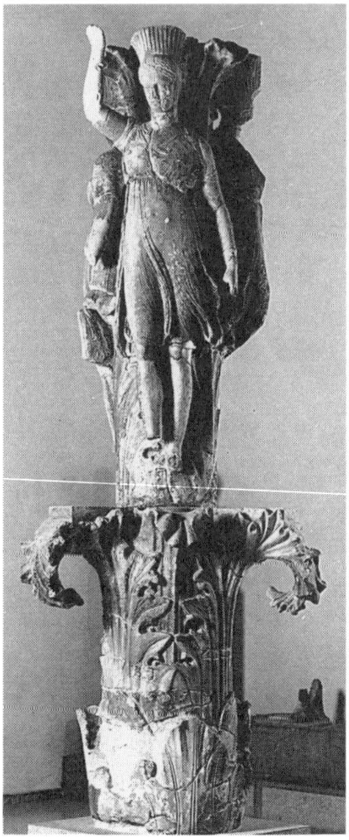

11. Dancers column, from Delphi. Ca. 375 B.C.

Skopas with his fire and emotion seems to be a never-ending subject for scholarly investigation. Andrew Stewart's 1977 study[51] has been extended both by himself and by others. In a monograph published by the Getty Museum,[52] Stewart erroneously espoused the authenticity of the de Bry head, reputedly bought by the Getty for $2.5m in 1979, and connected it with the Tegea pedimental fragments. 'It must be authentic because the comparisons with the Tegea heads are so close,' cries one. 'It must be a forgery because the comparisons with the Tegea heads are too close,' cries another. Polemic concerned with authentic versus fake is exciting to observe from the sidelines, but it can only be engaged in by those who handle the material in question. Other works by Skopas that have been studied recently include the Pothos figure (maybe part of a group with Aphrodite), the Hygieia, and the Hope Herakles.[53] Euphranor has been given a thorough study by Olga Palagia.[54] He was the only artist who had a reputation both as a sculptor and as a painter, and he wrote on proportion and colours. He was noted for the dignity and grandeur of his images – a reactionary and sober classicist with no statues of Eros, Aphrodite or satyrs to his name. A fragmentary Apollo, all that remains of the cult statue that once stood in the temple of Apollo Patroos on the west side of the Athenian Agora, seems to be his, and Palagia wishes to allot him the bronze Athena from the Piraeus (see p. 19 above), but others have disagreed and wish to give him the larger of the two Artemis figures from the same find.[55]

Euphranor has been seen as a precursor of Lysippos in his experiments with apparent proportions. The Getty Bronze (Colour Plate 2)[56] has been linked with the name of Lysippos, but with little hard fact; our understanding of Lysippos' style is still too hazy to bear such a burden.[57] What we have is a young man of the late fourth century – a prince? a victorious athlete? – a figure certainly that is moving into the more complex figuration that is a hallmark of Hellenistic.

NOTES

1. P. Bruneau, 'Sur l'origine supposée délienne des bronzes du Pirée, *BCH* 111 (1987), 342. Cf. what A. M. Snodgrass says about our acceptance of known settlement destructions ('positivist fallacy') in *An Archaeology of Greece* (California, 1987), pp. 37–8. For the study of Greek sculpture as the product of an anonymous craft, see R. Carpenter, *Greek Sculpture* (Chicago, 1960).

2. For general works on Archaic sculpture, see B. S. Ridgway, *The Archaic Style in Greek Sculpture* (Princeton, 1977) and Boardman *GSAP*.

3. *Kouroi, Archaic Greek Youths* (3rd edition, London, 1970; reprinted by Hakker, 1988) and *Korai, Archaic Greek Maidens* (London, 1968).

4. *AJA* 82 (1978), 461–72 (proportions of kouroi); 85 (1981), 269–80 (proportions of korai); 86 (1982), 173–82 (profiles of korai); 89 (1985), 399–409 (profiles of kouroi); 91 (1987), 287 (modern Olympics). For another close analysis, see I. Kleeman, *Frühe Bewegung* I *Grundzüge der Anlage von Bewegung* (Mainz, 1984).

5. A. M. Snodgrass, *Archaic Greece, the age of experiment* (London, 1980), p. 179.

6. 'When is a kouros not an Apollo? The Tenea "Apollo" revisited', *Corinthiaca, Studies in honor of Darrell A. Amyx*, ed. Mario A. Del Chiaro (Columbia, 1986), pp. 54–70; and review of *AKGP*, *AJA* 92 (1988), 610–11 (quotations from 60 and 610). See also on patronage L. A. Schneider, *Zu sozialen Bedeutung der archaischen Korenstatuen* (Hamburg, 1975).

7. 'Of kouroi and korai, Attic variety', *Hesperia* Supplement 20 (1982), 118–27.

8. See J. G. Pedley, *Greek Sculpture of the Archaic Period: the Island Workshops* (Mainz, 1976) and 'Cycladic influence in the sixth century sculpture of Attica', *Athens Comes of Age: from Solon to Salamis*, ed. W. A. P. Childs (Princeton, 1978), pp. 53–71. See also 'A group of early sixth century korai and the workshop of Chios', *AJA* 86 (1982), 183–91, pls. 22–5, and K.

Sheedy, 'The Delian Nike and the search for Chian sculpture', *AJA* 89 (1985), 619–26, pl. 67, 3–4 (a mirage). See also *Chios, a conference at the Homereion in Chios 1984*, edd. J. Boardman and C. E. Vaphopoulou-Richardson (Oxford, 1986). *AKGP* I has many contributions on the subject of regional origins and characteristics.

9. S. Kane, 'An archaic kore from Cyrene', *AJA* 84 (1980), 182–3, pls. 27–8; B. A. Barletta, 'The draped kouros type and the workshop of the Syracuse youth', *AJA* 91 (1987), 233–46.

10. 'Couroi argiens à Delphes', *BCH* Supplement 4 (1977), 13–22; 'Monuments votifs de Delphes. V. Les couroi d'Argos', *BCH* 106 (1982), 509–25 (quotation from 524). The sculptors are read as Polymedes and Theodotos, Argives.

11. J. R. Marszal, 'An architectural function for the Lyons kore', *Hesperia* 57 (1988), 203–6, pl. 56.

12. J. M. Hurwit, 'The Kritios boy: discovery, reconstruction and date', *AJA* 93 (1989), 41–80.

13. *GettyMJ* 14 (1986), 179–80 and M. True, 'A kouros at the Getty Museum', *Burlington Magazine* 129 (1987), 3–11. Now illustrated in Stewart, *Greek Sculpture* (see I, n. 8), figs. 133 and 135. See the *Connoisseur* May 1987 and *The Burlington Magazine* September 1990 for the case against authenticity. Cf. also the archaic grave relief which has been thought not to be original, J. Frel, *Death of a Hero* (Malibu, 1984). G. M. A. Richter's *Archaic Gravestones of Attica* (London, 1961) was reprinted in 1988 by the Bristol Classical Press.

14. H. Kyrieleis, *Führer durch das Heraion von Samos* (Athens, 1981), 45, fig. 32 and 'Neue archaische Skulpturen aus dem Heraion von Samos', *AKGP* I, pp. 35–45, pls. 14–22. The kore and kouros are now illustrated in Stewart, *Greek Sculpture* (I, n. 8), figs. 94 and 96, and 100 and 102. The Louvre Cheramyes: Boardman *GSAP* fig. 87.

15. Stewart in *Corinthiaca* (n. 6 above), p. 64, n. 48, suggests that the kouros makes a pair with the fragments, Richter, *Kouroi* (n. 3 above), nos. 24, 25 and 79, all from one kouros.

16. H. Payne and G. M. Young, *Archaic Marble Sculpture from the Acropolis* (London, 1936), pp. 4–9, 18–21. See Boardman *GSAP* figs. 114–5.

17. A. F. Stewart, 'Aristion', *AAA* 9 (1976), 257–66. The initial publication of Phrasikleia was by E. Mastrokostas, *AAA* 5 (1972), 298–324; a full publication is still awaited. For the Anavyssos kouros, Phrasikleia, and Theseus and Antiope, see Boardman *GSAP* figs. 107, 108a, and 205.2.

18. For Antenor's kore, see Boardman *GSAP* fig. 141, and for a figure from the east pediment of the Apollo temple at Delphi, and for a Victory akroterion, see figs. 142 and 204. E. Touloupa (III, n. 5) connects the Eretria pediment with him. J. Dörig, 'La tête Webb, l'Harmodios d'Anténor et le problème des copies romaines d'après des chefs-d'oeuvre archaïques', *AK* 12 (1969), 41–50, pls. 25–8, has suggested that the Webb head in the British Museuem (Boardman *GSAP* fig. 143), a rare Roman copy of an archaic piece, is from Antenor's Tyrantslayers group.

19. 'Alkamenes at Olympia', *BICS* 31 (1984), 199–211, pls. 10–12. It is based on B. Ashmole's work in *JHS* 56 (1936), 249 and *PBA* 48 (1962), 213–33, esp. 216. For Euthydikos' kore and the Blond Boy, see Boardman *GSAP* figs. 160 and 148, and for the Olympia material and a copy of the Hermes before the Gates, see Boardman *GSCP* fig. 21 (west pediment) and 189. For a recent discussion of Hermes as herm, see R. Osborne. 'The erection and mutilation of the Hermai', *PCPS* 211 (1985), 47—73.

20. For the origin and essence of the Classical style, see B. Ashmole. *The Classical Ideal in Greek Sculpture* (Cincinnati, 1962) and C. H. Hallett, 'The origins of the classical style in sculpture', *JHS* 106 (1986), 71–84, pls. 4–6. For recent general works on Classical sculpture, see B. S. Ridgway, *The Severe Style in Greek Sculpture* (Princeton, 1970) and *Fifth-Century Styles in Greek Sculpture* (Princeton, 1981), and Boardman *GSCP*. See also J. J. Pollitt, 'Early Classical Greek art in a Platonic universe', *Greek Art. Archaic into Classical, a Symposium held at the University of Cincinnati April 2–3, 1982*, ed. C. G. Boulter (Leiden, 1985), pp. 96–111, pls. 79–96.

21. On bronzes, see C. C. Mattusch, *Bronze Workers in the Athenian Agora* (Princeton, 1982); C. Houser and D. Finn, *Greek Monumental Bronze Sculpture* (London, 1983); P. C. Bol, *Antike Bronzetechnik, Kunst und Handwerk antiker Erzbilder* (Munich, 1985); C. Rolley, *Greek Bronzes*, trans. Roger Howell (London, 1986); C. C. Mattusch, *Greek Bronze Statuary, from the beginnings through the fifth century* (Cornell University Press, 1988). See also B. A. Sparkes,

'Greek Bronzes', *Greece & Rome* 34 (1987), 152–68. C. Rolley has published a running critique of recent publications in *RA* 1983, 325–36; 1985, 277–96; 1986, 377–91; 1987, 335–60; 1988, 341–55; 1989, 343–56. Close study of well-established pieces sometimes shows them to be different from what they had seemed. The Piombino statue, long considered a masterpiece of the early fifth century, has been shown by Ridgway to be a late pastiche, see *AntPl* 7 (Berlin, 1967), 43–75, pls. 24–34.

22. C. Landwehr, *Die antiken Gypsabgüsse aus Baiae* (Archäologische Forschungen 14, Berlin, 1985). See also W.-H. Schuchhardt and C. Landwehr, 'Statuenkopien der Tyrannenmörder-Gruppe', *JDAI* 101 (1986), 82–126 on copies of the Tyrantslayers.

23. It is the Marmor Parium that gives 477/6 B.C for the later group – not an unimpeachable source.

24. For the Piraeus Apollo, see Boardman *GSAP* fig. 150. G. Dontas, '*Ο χάλκινος Απόλλων του Πειραιά*', *AKGP* I, pp. 181–92, pls. 77–79. For the Delos connection, see 'La grande Artémis du Pirée: une oeuvre d'Euphranor', *AK* 25 (1982), 15–34, pls. 3–6.

25. For the Delphi Charioteer and inscription, see Boardman *GSCP* fig. 34.

26. For the Motya youth, see V. Tusa, 'Il Giovane di Mozia', *AKGP* II, pp. 1–11, pls. 82–5; N. Bonacasa and A. Buttitta (edd.), *La statua marmorea di Mozia e la scultura di stile severo in Sicilia, Atti della Giornata di Studio, Marsala, 1 Giugno, 1986* (Instituto di Archeologia, Universita di Palermo, Studi e Materiali 8, Rome, 1988); R. J. A. Wilson in *Archaeological Reports 1987–88*, 149–50; S. Moscati (ed.), *The Phoenicians* (Milan, 1988), pp. 538–41, with three colour illustrations.

27. For the Zeus of Artemisium, see Boardman *GSCP* fig. 35. R. Wünsche, 'Ergänzungsversuche am "Gott aus dem Meer" ', *AK* 21 (1978), 107, pl. 31 and 'Der "Gott aus dem Meer" ', *JDAI* 94 (1979), 77–111. For a study of the female figures, see R. Tölle-Kastenbein, *Frühklassische Peplosfiguren: Originale* (Mainz, 1980) and *Frühklassische Peplosfiguren: Typen und Repliken* (*AntPl* 20, Berlin, 1986).

28. For the Porticello head, see Boardman *GSCP* fig. 37. For a discussion, see B. S. Ridgway, 'The Bronzes from the Porticello Wreck', *AKGP* II, pp. 59–69, pls. 100–101 and for the wreck and its contents, C. J. Eiseman and B. S. Ridgway, *The Porticello Shipwreck: a Mediterranean merchant vessel of 415–385 B.C.* (Texas A&M University Press, 1987); quotations from p. 106. The date of the wreck should be earlier, ca. 430 B.C., see D. W. J. Gill, 'The date of the Porticello shipwreck: some observations on the Attic bolsals', *IJNA* 16 (1987), 31–3.

29. For the Themistokles head, see Boardman *GSCP* fig. 246. For discussion, see A. Linfert, *AntPl* 7 (Berlin, 1967), 87–94, pls. 39–46; Robertson *HGA*, pp. 187–8; B. S. Ridgway, *The Severe Style in Greek Sculpture* (Princeton, 1970), p. 105 and *Fifth Century Styles in Greek Sculpture* (Princeton, 1981), p. 179. And see M. I. Finley's comments, 'In lieblicher Bläue', *Arion* n.s. 3 (1976), 86–8.

For portraits in general, see G. M. A. Richter, *Portraits of the Greeks*, 2nd ed., abridged and revised by R. R. R. Smith (Oxford, 1984); J. Frel, *Greek Portraits* (Malibu, 1981); J. Dörig, 'Quelques remarques sur l'origine ionienne du portrait grec', *Eikones*, 89–95; K. Schefold, 'Die Überlieferung der griechischen Bildniskunst', *Praestant Interna*, 79–90; B. A. Sparkes, *So few people look like themselves* (Southampton, 1987); K. Fittschen (ed.), *Griechische Porträts* (Darmstadt, 1988). For some recent discussions about sixth century realism, see U. Sinn, 'Beobachtungen zum "Realismus" in der Grossplastik des 6. Jhs v. Chr.', *AM* 98 (1983), 25–43, pls. 5–10; F. Eckstein, '*τὰ ὦτα κατεηγότα*', *AJA* 89 (1985), 613–7, pl. 67, 1–2; E. Akurgal, 'Neue Archaische Skulpturen aus Anatolien', *AKGP* I, pp. 9–14, pls. 4–5 (? a satrap head from Herakleia Pontica, ca. 530 B.C.; cf. the well known Sabouroff head, Boardman, *GSAP* figs. 113 and 133).

30. For the Riace bronzes, see Boardman *GSCP* figs. 38–9. See also A. Busignani, *Gli Eroi di Riace* (Florence, 1981); *Bollettino d'Arte*, 3 series speciale, *Due Bronzi di Riace: Rinvenimento, restauro, analisi ed ipotesi di interpretazione* (1985) – see the review by J. Marcadé, 'Rapports techniques et publications archéologiques: à propos des bronzes de Riace', *RA* 1986, 89–100.

31. For Kresilas, see Busignani (n. 30 above); for Myron and Alkamenes, see G. Dontas, 'Considerazioni sui bronzi di Riace: proposte sui maestri e sulla provenienza dell statue', *Bollettino d'Arte* (n. 30 above), 277–96; for Onatas, see O. Deubner, 'Die Statuen von Riace', *JDAI* 103 (1988), 127–53.

32. See W. Fuchs, 'Zu den Grossbronzen von Riace', *Boreas* 4 (1981), 25–28 and 'Zu den

Grossbronzen von Riace', *Praestant Interna*, 34–40. J. Barron is working on the Riace bronzes and Pheidias (see next note).

33. For the Athena Lemnia, see Boardman *GSCP* fig. 183 and p. 84 for a mention of Barron's theory. For Pheidias' Athenas, see A. Linfert, 'Athenen des Pheidias', *AM* 97 (1982), 57–77, pls. 17–21.

34. 'Lemnia and Lemnos: sidelights on a Pheidian Athena', *Kanon*, 101–7, pls. 29–30. Harrison chooses the Athena Medici for the Lemnia. For other discussion of the Furtwängler Lemnia, see K. J. Hartwick, 'The Athena Lemnia reconsidered', *AJA* 87 (1983), 336–46, pls. 42–6 and O. Palagia, ' *'Ερύθημα . . . ἀντὶ κράνους* – in defence of Furtwängler's Athena Lemnia', *AJA* 91 (1987), 81–4.

35. 'Two Pheidian heads: Nike and Amazon', *Eye of Greece*, pp. 53–65, pls. 14–16.

36. For the moulds and workshop, see A. Mallwitz and W. Schiering, *Die Werkstatt des Pheidias in Olympia* (Olympische Forschungen 5, Berlin, 1964) and A. Mallwitz, *Olympia und seine Bauten* (Munich, 1972), 255–66. For the late fifth-century vase, see B. B. Shefton, 'The krater from Baksy', *Eye of Greece*, pp. 149–81, pls. 41–48. For the Niobids, see C. Vogelpohl, 'Die Niobiden vom Thron des Zeus in Olympia', *JDAI* 95 (1980), 197–226.

37. J. Dörig, *La Frise est de l'Héphaisteion* (Mainz, 1985) gives the work to Myron. There has been discussion about the Athena and Marsyas group, see G. Daltrop, *Il gruppo mironiano di Atene e Marsia nei Musei Vaticani* (Vatican, 1980) and G. Daltrop and P. C. Bol, *Athena des Myron* (Frankfurt, 1983). For a critical look at the group, see H. A. Weis, 'The "Marsyas" of Myron: old problems and new evidence', *AJA* 83 (1979), 214–9, pls. 30–31.

38. For one copy of the Perikles head, see Boardman *GSCP* fig. 188. D. Pandermalis, *Untersuchungen zu den klassischen Strategenköpfen* (Freiburg, 1969); E. B. Harrison, *Eye of Greece*, pp. 82–4. See also B. Ridgway, *Roman Copies* (I, n. 11), pp. 55–6.

39. C. C. Vermeule, *Polykleitos* (Boston, 1969); T. Lorenz, *Polyklet* (Wiesbaden, 1972); H. von Steuben, *Der Kanon des Polyklet* (Tübingen, 1973); R. Tobin, 'The canon of Polykleitos', *AJA* 79 (1975), 307–21; A. F. Stewart, 'The canon of Polykleitos: a question of evidence', *JHS* 98 (1978), 122–31; E. Berger, 'Zum von Plinius (N.H. 34, 55) überlieferten "nudus talo incessens" des Polyklet', *AK* 21 (1978), 55–62. Amazons: B. S. Ridgway, 'The story of five Amazons', *AJA* 78 (1974), 1–17, pls. 1–4; M. Weber, 'Die Amazonen von Ephesos I', *JDAI* 91 (1976), 28–96; 'Die Amazonen von Ephesos II', *JDAI* 99 (1984), 75–126; 'Klassische Amazonen als Gemmenbilder', *Kanon*, 134–9, pls. 39–40; E. B. Harrison, *Eye of Greece*, pp. 65–88, pls. 17–22; K. J. Hartwick, 'The so-called Ephesus Amazon', *JDAI* 101 (1986), 127–36.

40. For the Prokne and Itys, see Boardman *GSCP* fig. 135 and M. S. Bruskari, *The Acropolis Museum, a descriptive catalogue* (Athens, 1974), pp. 165–6, fig. 351. See also H. Knell, *AntPl* 17 (Berlin, 1978), 9–19, pls. 1–9; E. La Rocca, 'Prokne ed Itys sull'Acropolis: una motivazione per la Dedica', *AM* 101 (1986), 153–66. For a general treatment of Alkamenes, see W.-H. Schuchhardt, *Alkamenes* (Berlin, 1977).

41. J. Carter, 'Prokne and Sophokles' *AJA* 85 (1981), 189, picking up a suggestion by Robertson *HGA*, pp. 286–7. See also E. B. Harrison's investigation of the evidence for the cult statues Alkamenes made for the Hephaisteion (not the temple we know by that name), 'Alkamenes' sculptures for the Hephaisteion', *AJA* 81 (1977), 137–78, 265–87, 411–26.

42. For the Sosianus temple, see III, nn. 38–40.

43. *Eye of Greece*, pp. 53–65, pls. 14–15.

44. G. Despinis, *Συμβολὴ στὴν μελέτην τοῦ ἔργου τοῦ 'Αγορακρίτου* (Athens, 1971) and *Ergon* 1977, 12–14. B. Petrakos, 'La base de la Némésis d'Agorakrite', *BCH* 105 (1981), 227–53 and '*Προβλήματα της βάσης του αγάλματος της Νεμέσεως*', *AKGP* II, pp. 89–107, pls. 111–16. For a later copy of the cult statue that can be recognized, see Boardman *GSCP* fig. 122. For a possible original late fifth-century cult statue of a goddess (South Italy?), see *GettyMJ* 17 (1989), 110 (2 metres high, of marble and limestone). For a brief general statement on cult idols, see I. B. Romano, 'Early Greek idols', *Expedition* 24 (1982), 3–13.

45. G. B. Waywell, 'Athena Mattei', *BSA* 66 (1971), 373–82, pls. 66–72.

46. S. Adam, *The Technique of Greek Sculpture* (London, 1966), 124–8, pls. 70–72.

47. 'Pausanias and Praxiteles', *Hesperia* Supplement 20 (1982), 182–91.

48. K. D. Morrow, *Greek Footwear and the Dating of Sculpture* (The University of Wisconsin Press, 1985), pp. 83–4.

49. For the Dancing Maidens, see Robertson *HGA*, pp. 406–7 and 691, n. 122.

50. C. Vatin, 'Les danseuses de Delphes', *CRAI* 1983, 26–40; L. Robert, 'Bulletin épigraphique', *REG* 97 (1984), 44, no. 214; P. Cartledge, 'In their own write: literacy in ancient Greece', *Pegasus* 31 (1988), 23–8, esp. 27. Dating of the monument has varied: B. S. Ridgway, *Roman Copies* (I, n. 11), 39 and 46, n. 11 dated it after the earthquake of 373 B.C. and J. Frel, 'Le sculpteur des danseuses', *GettyMJ* 6/7 (1978–79), 75–82, put the figures in the 330s.

51. A. F. Stewart, *Skopas of Paros* (Park Ridge, 1977).

52. A. F. Stewart, *Skopas in Malibu* (Malibu, 1982). Stewart now considers the head a modern forgery (see *Greek Sculpture* (I, n. 8), p. 345).

53. R. Lattimore, 'Two statues of Herakles', *GettyMJ* 2 (1975), 17–26; 'Skopas and the Pothos', *AJA* 91 (1987), 411–20. For Tegea, see recently A. Delivorrias and A. Linfert, '*ΣΚΟΠΑΔΙΚΑ* II: la statue d'Hygie dans la temple d'Alea à Tégée', *BCH* 107 (1983), 277–88; N. J. Norman, 'The temple of Athena Alea at Tegea', *AJA* 88 (1984), 169–94, pls. 29–31 and 'Asklepios and Hygieia and the cult statue at Tegea', *AJA* 90 (1986), 425–30. See also O. Palagia, 'The Hope Herakles reconsidered', *OJA* 3 (1984), 107–26 (a pastiche, not a Roman copy of a Skopas statue). For Skopas on Samothrace, see P. W. Lehmann, *Skopas in Samothrace* (Northampton, 1973). For the Mausoleum, see pp. 35–37.

54. '*Εὐφράνορος τέχνη*', *AAA* 6 (1973), 323–9 and *Euphranor* (Leiden, 1980).

55. G. Dontas, 'La grande Artémis du Pirée: une oeuvre d'Euphranor', *AK* 25 (1982), 15–34, pls. 3–6, and 'Ein verkanntes Meisterwerk im Nationalmuseum von Athen. Der Marmorkopf *Γ*. 177 und Überlegungen zum Stil Euphranors', *Himmelmann Festschrift*, pp. 143–50, pls. 27–8.

56. J. Frel, *The Getty Bronze* (2nd edition, Malibu, 1982).

57. E. Sjöqvist, *Lysippos* (Cincinnati, 1966); P. Moreno, *Testimonianze per le teoria artistica di Lisippo* (Treviso, 1973) and *Lisippo* I (Bari, 1974); A. F. Stewart, 'Lysippos and Hellenistic sculpture', *AJA* 87 (1983), 262. For the Hellenistic period, see now J. J. Pollitt, *Art in the Hellenistic Age* (Cambridge, 1986).

III. ARCHITECTURAL SCULPTURE

The erection of a building – be it temple, treasury, colonnade, or theatre – argues commitment, means, and purpose, and the architectural sculpture that adorned the religious buildings is likely to have had programmatic intent, whether religious or political. The very complexity of the undertaking, and the limitation of the shapes decorated, have been seen as generating forces behind the development of advances in archaic sculpture. This is Anthony Snodgrass's antithesis to the position he maintains about the production of kouroi and korai (see p. 10 above): 'It is the pedimental figures which should be held up as examples of the attainment of Archaic sculptors . . . their adventurousness in pose and subject was the biggest contribution of the age to later sculpture.'[1]

Archaic

Already in the early sixth century the pediment from the Artemis temple on Corfu with Medusa and Perseus has been shown to convey complex messages. The subjects have not only been interpreted in terms of the inspiration of religious awe ('it is essentially monitory (directed to human beings) rather than minatory (to bogeys)'), but it has also been seen to represent a stage in development from apotropaic to narrative and dramatic, with the addition of Perseus and Chrysaor bringing political overtones from Corinth.[2] Similarly, the mid-sixth-century pediments on the Athenian Akropolis have been thought to reflect the interests of the tyrants, propaganda for Peisistratos and his sons: Herakles versus Triton, Herakles' Introduction into Olympus, his struggle against the Hydra. It has even been suggested that some of the smaller pediments could have decorated 'palace' buildings on the rock.[3]

Late-Archaic temples and treasuries have been studied for their dates and for their interpretation. Some would see the Athenian Treasury at Delphi with its metopes of Theseus and Herakles[4] in the context of the years after 499 B.C. when Athens made a strike against Persian control at Ephesos and Sardis, and in mythological terms Theseus took part in Herakles' eastern adventures. Theseus also figures in the West pediment of the Apollo Daphnephoros temple at Eretria[5] and his battle versus the Amazons is once again considered in the context of contemporary events against the Persians. The Aegina pediments are also subject for argument. With the restorations removed, they can be seen more clearly, and work at the site is raising questions of date that will need resolution.[6]

Early Classical

The sculptures from the Zeus temple at Olympia, the only major temple construction that we know of for the second quarter of the fifth century, have been admired for the grandeur of their conception and for their superb workmanship.[7] Much attention has been paid to the masters behind the design. Pausanias' mention (5.10.8) of Alkamenes of Athens for the West pediment and Paionios of Mende for the East, both sculptors known to have been working in the late fifth century, has always caused controversy. Ascription to Paionios may be explained by confusion in Pausanias' notes between the Victory figures on the akroteria (perhaps added later) and the pediment. With Paionios thus removed, the way may be open for one master for both pediments, and one recent suggestion is that the man is Alkamenes, but not the sculptor still working at the end of the century, but an older sculptor of the same name, perhaps a grandfather (see pp. 12–13 above). The Athenian connection is certainly present in the West pediment. For whereas the metopes concern Herakles, the founder of the games, and the East pediment centres round the local king Oinomaos, the West pediment not only has stylistic and iconographic affinities with Athenian work (the paintings in the Theseion, an Athenian version of the battle against the centaurs, and reflections of the Tyrantslayers group in Athens) but is charged with political propaganda: Theseus, anti-Spartan; resistance of the Pisatans and others to the synoikism of the Eleians in 471/470 B.C., etc.[8] It is suggested that the Eleian authorities specifically chose to compliment Athens and invited Alkamenes and his team of craftsmen to carry out the work.

Classical

The next half-century belongs to Athens. The Athenian Akropolis in its classical phase[9] still holds a central place in the study of Greek art, and there is much that is new to extract from the broken stones. Modern industrial methods of manufacture have cast a pall over Athens, the dreaded *nefos*, and have necessitated radical solutions to the decaying buildings of the Akropolis. Preservation of the very stones has become paramount, so that the Erechtheion caryatids and the remaining pedimental figures of the Parthenon are now replaced by replicas.[10] A cast museum is being established on the southern side of the Akropolis, whilst the Elgin marbles remain in London. The debate over their future continues.[11]

In the midst of all this rescue work and polemic, academic study advances apace – indeed, Parthenon studies are once again a growth area. It is still possible to recognize new fragments that belong to the sculptures and to make joins. An exhaustive inventory is being compiled of all the fragments that are to be found on top of the rock and on its slopes. Recently A. Mantis, working in the Akropolis Museum, has shown a fine eye for detail, and some metope blocks (Fig. 13) and other carvings have benefited from his researches by the addition of vital fragments.[12] Equally important has been the work of Ernst Berger in Basel, now a major centre for Parthenon studies, with a cast gallery (Fig. 12) that has enabled new theories to be tested.[13]

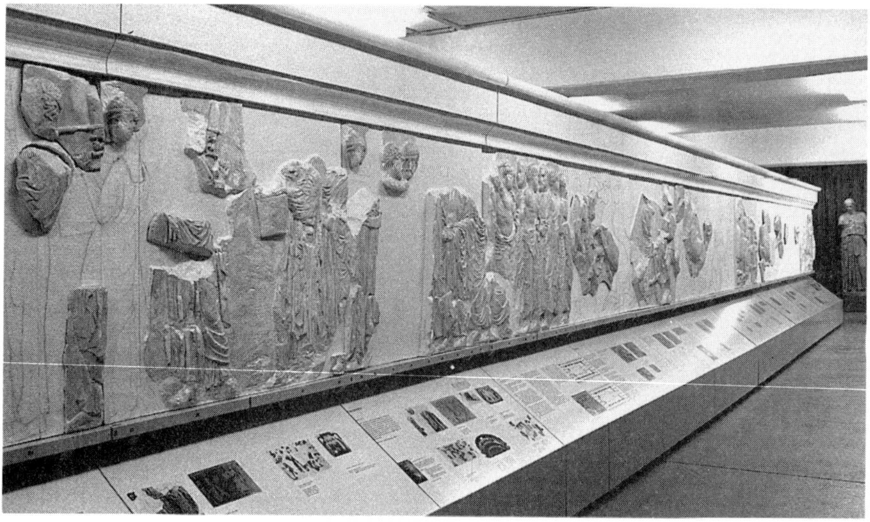

12. The Parthenon exhibition room, Basel.

The casts are made of a light styrofoam, large blocks of which can be manhandled and thus placed in varying possible arrangements. This has enabled a complete set of casts of sculptural fragments and pediment floors to be brought together, and new full-size groupings have been tried. A conference in Basel in 1982 brought together many scholars and ideas, and further advances have been made since then.[14] An indispensible tool of scholarship is Frank Brommer's now complete trio of volumes on the architectural sculpture of metopes, pediments, and frieze.[15]

The metopes have attracted attention, and, being earliest from the point of view of style and construction, they are open to suggestions that they belong to an earlier version of the temple.[16] Those on the East and West ends have suffered much from pollution, and it is necessary to study old photographs and casts to help out the now crumbling blocks. There is still controversy over the identification of the Western series: Greeks versus Amazons or versus Persians (the former more likely); and the Eastern series still provokes theories on divine identities.[17] There is much missing from the North and South sides; hence solutions are hard to find. The Northern series, with episodes from the Trojan War, are now seen to be less straightforward than had been supposed, whilst the Southern series still causes difficulty: 'no more stubborn problem . . . than the subject matter of the south metopes'.[18] Centaurs fight Lapiths at the feast at either side, with new fragments added to some with the help of the Carrey drawings of the seventeenth century (Fig. 13), but the missing centre (8 or 9 metopes) can only be studied in the drawings made by Carrey. Recent suggestions have favoured such subjects as an Attic story that combined with a centauromachy, Ixion, the early kings and heroes of Athens, Daidalos and Ikaros, Theseus and Ariadne. None of them makes the south side a totally homogeneous group, but the centaur fight would have been intolerably boring if repeated on all thirty-two metopes. Wesenberg's new theory has them originally intended for a location over the porches at the East and West ends where the frieze was eventually placed.

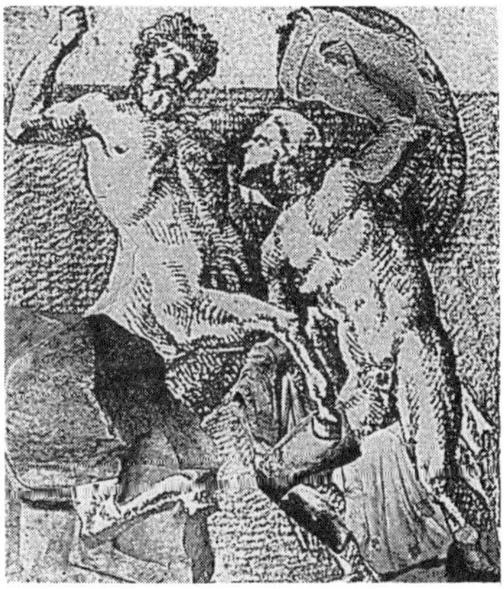
13. Metope S 11, the Parthenon. 440s B.C.

As for the pediments, it is common knowledge that one sentence in Pausanias (1.24.5) is all that we are told of their subject matter: 'As you go into the temple called the Parthenon, everything on the pediment has to do with the birth of Athena; the far side shows Poseidon quarrelling with Athena over the country.' Christian zeal and the Venetian bomb of A.D. 1687 have denied us direct knowledge of the central groups. The West pediment has been perceptively studied by Erika Simon who has shown that the moment depicted in the struggle was after the decision had gone to Athena, and Poseidon was on the attack.[19] The centre of the East pediment still exercises the ingenuity of scholars, and recent work in Basel is important here (Fig. 14).[20] Experiments with the placing of what we know of the central figures from Carrey's drawings and other evidence, have produced a vastly different arrangement from that usually reconstituted with the assistance of the Madrid altar. The central trio of Hera, Zeus, and Athena that the experiments create has been recognized on a late fifth-century Athenian red-figure krater (Fig. 15) that has other Pheidian associations.[21]

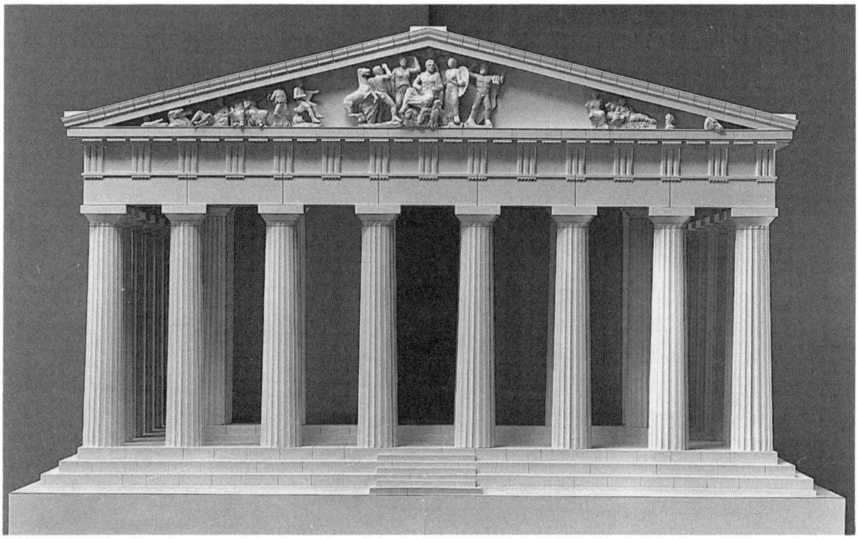

14. Model of the Parthenon, East end.

The frieze, which has no reference preserved from antiquity, continues to fascinate and to invite new interpretations.[22] John Boardman's theory[23] that the frieze celebrates Marathon, with the emphasis on heroic cavalry, and the gods and eponymous heroes waiting to receive thc heroized dead, has gained many adherents, though some see the mixture as producing too chaotic a result. Whereas Boardman stresses the unity of time and place by setting all the events in the Agora, others have dispersed the setting into such locations as the Attic plain, the Agora, and the Akropolis. Most would agree that this is no ordinary Panathenaia but differ in interpretation of detail: the groupings of riders on different sides are seen to refer to tribes and phratries, Kleisthenic and pre-Kleisthenic organizations; the ten eponymous heroes are thought to be eight archons with a marshal and a secretary; and the small figure holding the robe on the East frieze is by some considered female.[24] Concentration on the subject matter has perhaps deflected attention from the question of style. Frank Brommer maintains that we should not look for stylistic development as the whole frieze was designed and executed in too short a space of time; he also sees all the slabs being carved before being set in place,

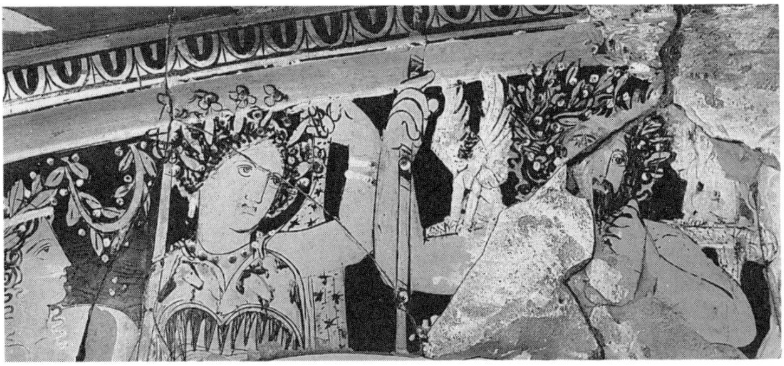

15. Fragment of an Attic red-figure bell-krater, from Baksy. Late fifth century B.C.

whereas most would see the North and South as carved in situ.[25] Robin Osborne in a refreshing view of the frieze as a whole considers the intended effect from the point of view of the spectators making their way outside the peristyle towards the Eastern entrance. From that angle the frieze is seen in small sections and moves the spectators to their final goal: a sight of the gold and ivory statue through the doorway. But perhaps more importantly Osborne urges us not to divorce style and subject matter, and he himself links the two; 'The Parthenon frieze . . . presents the very aristocratic image of Athenian democracy at its most élitist, where all citizens are not just soldiers but the quintessential soldier, the young man in the cavalry whom public inspection requires to be a model of physical fitness. In presenting this image the frieze also promotes it, for in showing all the heads without individualisation the frieze shows a citizen body where distinctions are abolished and all are equal, and where, despite widely varying personal circumstances, all may aspire to the same role; in involving the spectator in the procession the frieze draws the spectator to identify with the anonymous citizenry and share their aspirations.'[26]

The view of the East end of the Parthenon presented gods in the pediment, in the metopes, and in the frieze, and drew the eye to the interior where the base with another parade of gods underlay Pheidias' massive gold and ivory statue of Athena herself. The Toronto reconstruction (Colour Plate 1C) gives it a gaudiness and elaboration that are in keeping with what we know from literary references, and the original no doubt had the dazzling effect of expensive display that was intended.[27] It was heavily copied and adapted both in its entirety

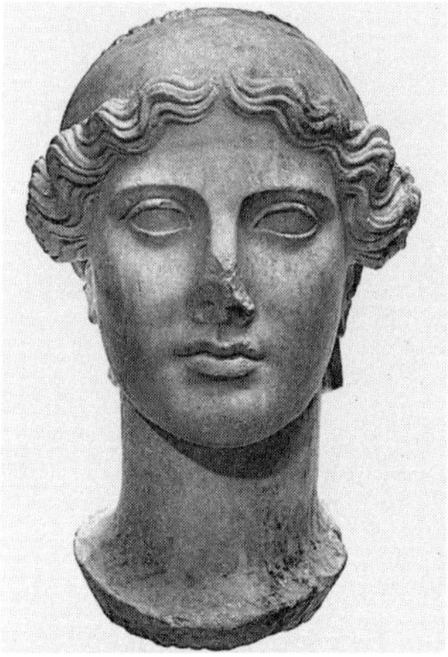

16. Marble head of Athena Parthenos' Victory. Copy of original of ca. 440 B.C.

at various sizes, and in its particulars – shield, sandals, base, and winged victory (Fig. 16) that stood on the right hand of Athena (see pp. 16–17 above). Eve Harrison's work on the shield which seems to have been one of the most copied elements, has produced a more complex and fuller design than that reconstituted by earlier scholars.[28]

The sculpture that adorned the temple and the statue that stood inside were all part of a programme of decoration that emphasized Athenian power under the protection of Athena. Some years ago Arthur Lawrence compared the form and function of the Akropolis with the Apadana at Persepolis,[29] and other scholars since have been prepared to see a conscious contrast between the two: democratic Athens versus imperialist Persia. More recently the connection between the two has been reinforced, but with a new slant.[30] It is suggested that the Parthenon frieze borrowed from and emulated Achaemenid Persian models. 'To the Athenians who planned the Parthenon frieze the sculpture was meant to convey something powerful and energizing: the harmonious ordering of a society guided by positivistic ideas and far-reaching aspirations. Part of the contemporary impact of its representational imagery derived from its calculated emulation of the programmatic imperial visions of Darius.' Such a radical view is unlikely to go unchallenged.

The sculptures of the other temples of Athens and Attica that belong to the second half of the fifth century have been studied singly and together. Of the four Doric temples that have been attributed by some to one architect (Hephaisteion; Ares temple from Acharnai; Poseidon temple, Sounion; and Nemesis temple, Rhamnous),[31] the Hephaisteion, if such it was, has had its fair share of theories with regard to the date, the designer, the style and the subject matter of the figured decoration and of the missing cult statues.[32] A date around 430–425 B.C. seems acceptable to most; two masters and three pupils (from Paros?) have been thought likely to account for the friezes, stylistically the work has been linked to the Ilissos temple material, but the subject matter is still unsolved. José Dörig's attempts to date the work to the mid century, to attribute it to Myron, to link the subject to the story of Erekhtheus and to have Euripides borrowing inspiration directly from the carving for his own *Erekhtheus*, have none of them commanded much of a following.[33] Of the three Ionic temples (Erekhtheion; Nike Apteros; Ilissos temple), the Erekhtheion has had its caryatids and their copies, and the frieze figures, studied in detail,[34] and the identity of the temple called into question,[35] and the dates of both the Nike and the Ilissos temple have come in for close consideration, with both on balance being placed in the 420s.[36] Eve Harrison has drawn attention to the way in which figure types on the Hephaisteion and on the Nike and Ilissos temples make use of groups from the Parthenos shield.[37] Within the short space of time that all this architectural decoration was being carved and erected in Athens, we should doubtless expect to find interweaving of subjects, styles, and composition.

The Parthenon sculptures suffered their diaspora in recent times, other temple sculptures were already dispersed in antiquity. In the heart of Rome stands the theatre of Marcellus, erected by Augustus for his favourite ('tu Marcellus eris', Vergil, *Aeneid* 6.883). Nearby are the remains of the temple of Apollo Medicus/Alexikakos.[38] It was vowed in 433 B.C. and dedicated in 431 B.C., and because it was a foreign cult (brought from Euboean Cumae), it was built outside the pomerium. It was rebuilt for the last time ca. 25 B.C. by C. Sosius and thus is named the temple of Apollo Sosianus – it had been the only temple to Apollo until Augustus' temple to Apollo was vowed in 36 B.C. and dedicated in 28 B.C. on the Palatine. Excavation in the area of the theatre of Marcellus in the 1930s brought to light fragments of earlier marble sculpture that was not recognized at the time as belonging to a temple pediment. Recently Eugenio La Rocca has made a study of the fragments,[39] stored in various museum basements in Rome, and has recreated a new pedimental set of architectural figures of Parian marble that are seen as originals of the decade 430–420 B.C. The influence of the Parthenon is clear, but they are unlikely to have been made in Athens; their origin may be in a Parian workshop.

La Rocca's composition identifies a flying Victory (Colour Plate 3) who has crowned Theseus (Fig. 17) with laurel during his struggle against the Amazons on horseback.[40] The hero's cloak falls from his left thigh, and his forelocks have been repaired with locks of bronze. Athena is present as the central figure of the pediment. La Rocca sees the subject as the joint expedition of Herakles and Theseus to Themiskyra, with the emphasis falling on the figure of Theseus being crowned by Victory. The pediment could certainly not have been made for a temple in Rome in the fifth century B.C., no matter how close the date of the original foundation of the Apollo Medicus temple may be to the set of sculptures. Rome at that time was not so advanced. The figures must have been plundered (the area was noted for the plundered works that were set up there) – but where from and when? La Rocca recalls the earlier kneeling Amazon archer from the temple of Apollo Daphnephoros ('crowned with laurel') at Eretria – it was part of the pedimental group that included the famous Theseus and Antiope, and Athena, and was discovered in Rome where it is thought to have been since antiquity. Were the later figures part of a composition that replaced the Theseus and Antiope pediment when that had been destroyed by the Persians in 490 B.C.? The central Athena figure is of the right size.

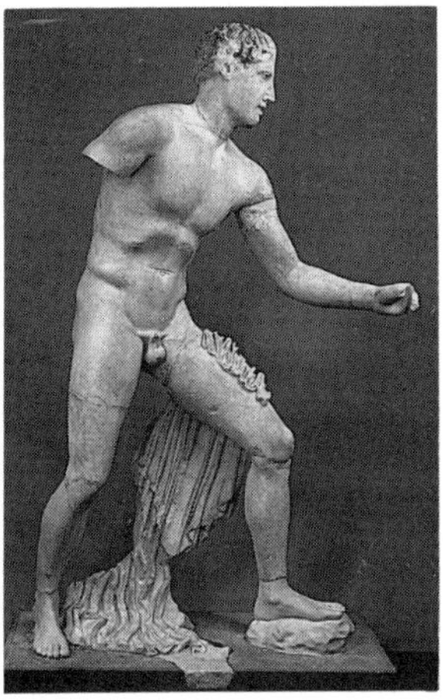

17. Theseus, from the Apollo Sosianus temple, Rome. Ca. 430 B.C.

Livy (32.16) tells of statuary plundered from Eretria and taken to Rome by L. Quinctius Flamininus in 198 B.C. La Rocca asks if Theseus versus the Amazon queen may have acted as a paradigm for Augustus against Cleopatra, with Rome as the new Athens. The case is not proved and is also connected with the chronological discussion that is taking place about the earlier group which some would wish to downdate to the period after the Persian attack.[41] Other evidence that needs to be taken into account is the set of Niobid figures being shot down by Apollo and Artemis, that were found in the gardens of Sallust and are now in the Terme Museum and in Copenhagen.[42] There is close similarity between the Copenhagen Niobid and the Sosian Hippolyte, and the date is once more around 440–430 B.C. In one passage (36.28), Pliny the Elder is notoriously confused about attribution: 'par haesitatio est in templo Apollinis Sosiani Niobae liberos morientes Scopas an Praxiteles fecerit' ('there is equal doubt whether Scopas or Praxiteles made the dying children of Niobe in the temple of Sosian Apollo'). Present study would suggest neither did but would ask whether the Amazonomachy and the Niobid pediments were both brought from the Apollo temple in Eretria and whether the Amazon battle was placed in the pediment and the Niobid figures arranged inside the temple. The prospect of a solution to the puzzle is exciting.

Fourth Century and After

The fourth century is no less fertile with architectural sculpture. The pediments and akroteria of the Asklepios temple at Epidauros (ca. 375 B.C.) are soon to be published in full by Nikolas Yalouris,[43] and it is reported that two hundred new fragments have been added which considerably alter all previous attempts at a reconstruction of the compositions. This was a progressive work, and it has been asked whether Skopas may not have served his apprenticeship on it. Yalouris has also worked on the material from the Apollo Epikourios temple at Bassai, and the sculptural decoration is now generally considered to belong to the very end of the fifth century.[44]

John Carter's work[45] on the seemingly unrewarding fragmentary remains of the Ionic Athena temple and altar at Priene shows that the coffer reliefs which depicted battles against Amazons and Giants belong to the original fourth century construction of the temple and can be connected with the frieze and coffer reliefs of the Mausoleum. The architect Pytheos seems to provide the connection, as the literary tradition links him as architect of the Priene temple, and as architect and sculptor earlier at Halikarnassos (Fig. 18). This more important structure continues to attract scholarly endeavour and is still proving a most daunting task. The recent Danish excavations under Kristian Jeppesen[46] are winning more precise information from the ground, and Geoffrey Waywell's publication of the freestanding figures (mostly in the British Museum)[47] has provided us with a much more realistic conception of the appearance of the whole building and of the disposition of the different categories of sculpture. It has also taught us to judge the importance of the frieze decoration against a much more impressive set of sculptures. The chariot team on top, the series of lions, the three friezes at different levels round the building, the figures in the round on six different levels and at three different scales (colossal standing and in action; heroic standing; and life-size battles – over three hundred figures in all) show how difficult it is to sort out the nature of the collaboration between designers and sculptors. The literary sources give us a fistful of names of leading sculptors of the day for such a big commission – Skopas, Bryaxis, Leokhares, Timotheos, Praxiteles (?), not to mention Satyros and the architect Pytheos – and modern scholars have been quick to see the design or hand of one or another on the small percentage of the remains. It is now thought that the major names may have worked on the freestanding podium figures only, not on the reliefs where the individual styles have usually been sought. That this is not a sterile occupation can be attributed to the attraction of searching for the

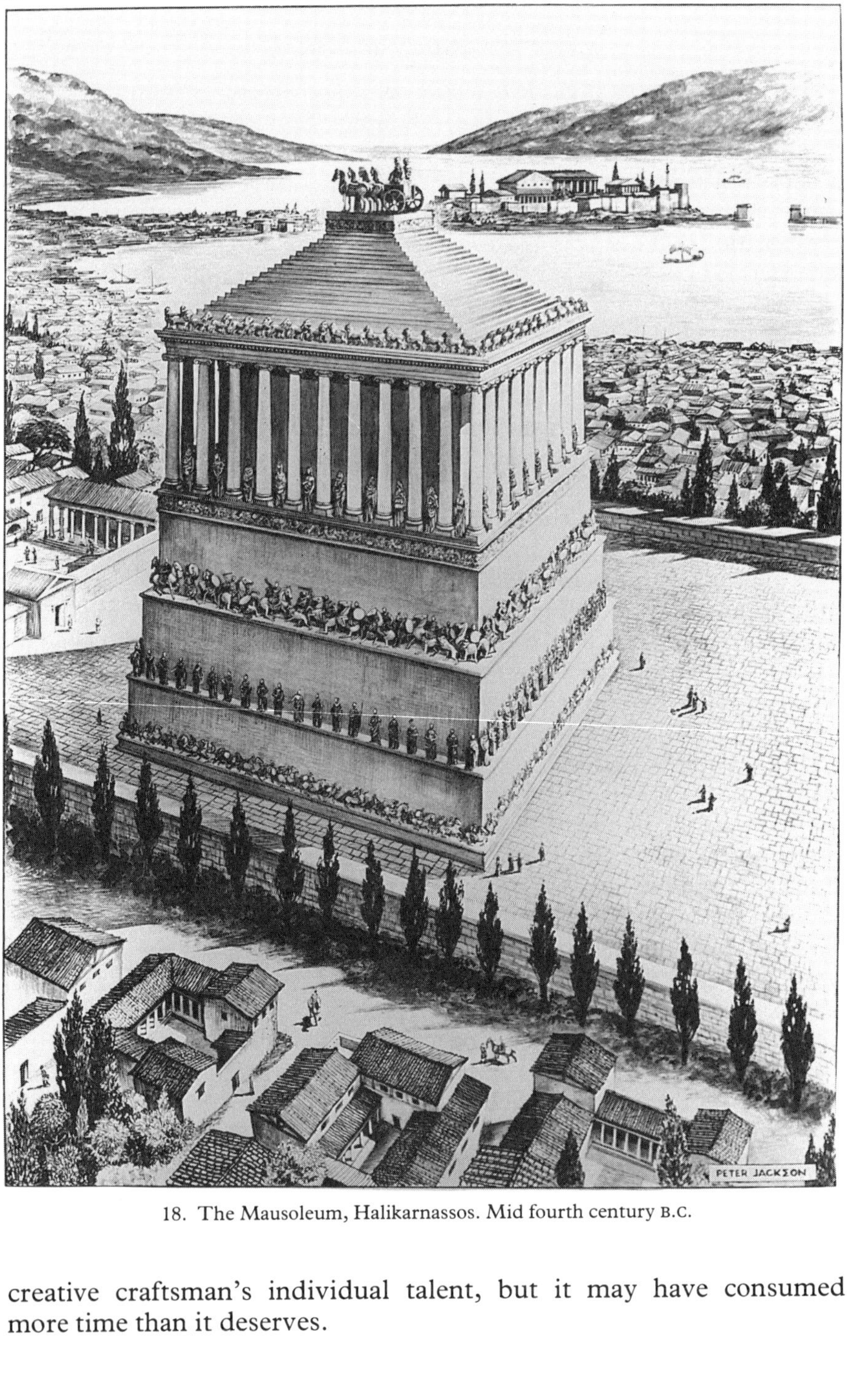

18. The Mausoleum, Halikarnassos. Mid fourth century B.C.

creative craftsman's individual talent, but it may have consumed more time than it deserves.

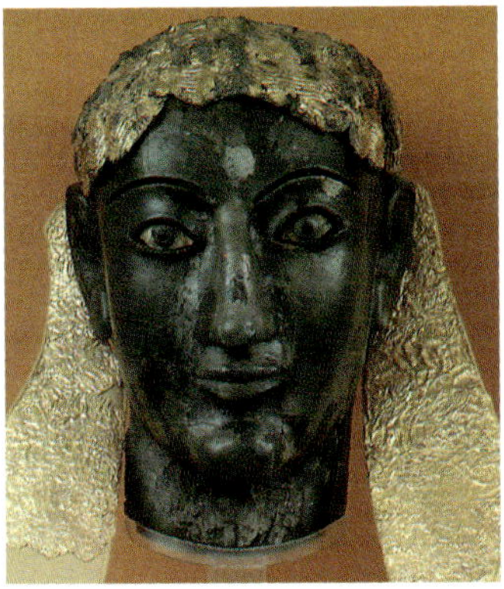

Plate 1A. Gold and ivory head of Apollo, from Delphi. 550-525 B.C. (See p.2)

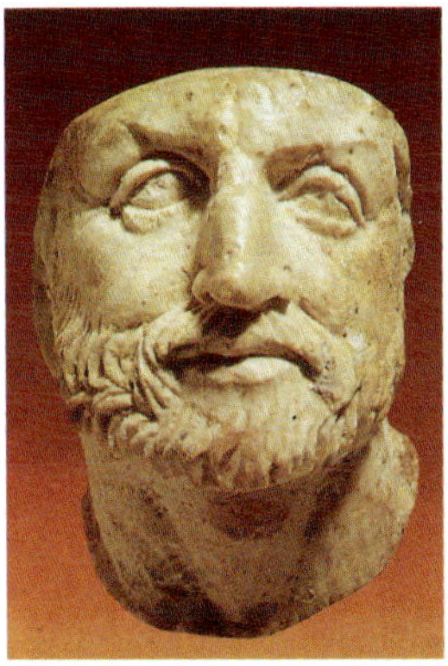

Plate 1B. Ivory head of Philip II of Macedon, from Vergina. Ca. 340 B.C. (See p.37)

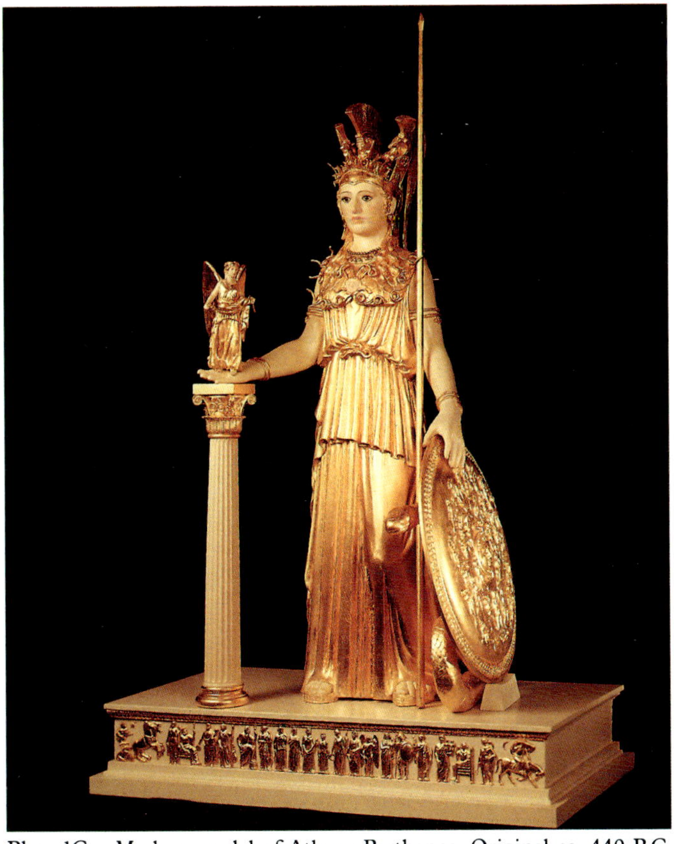

Plate 1C. Modern model of Athena Parthenos. Original ca. 440 B.C. (See p.31)

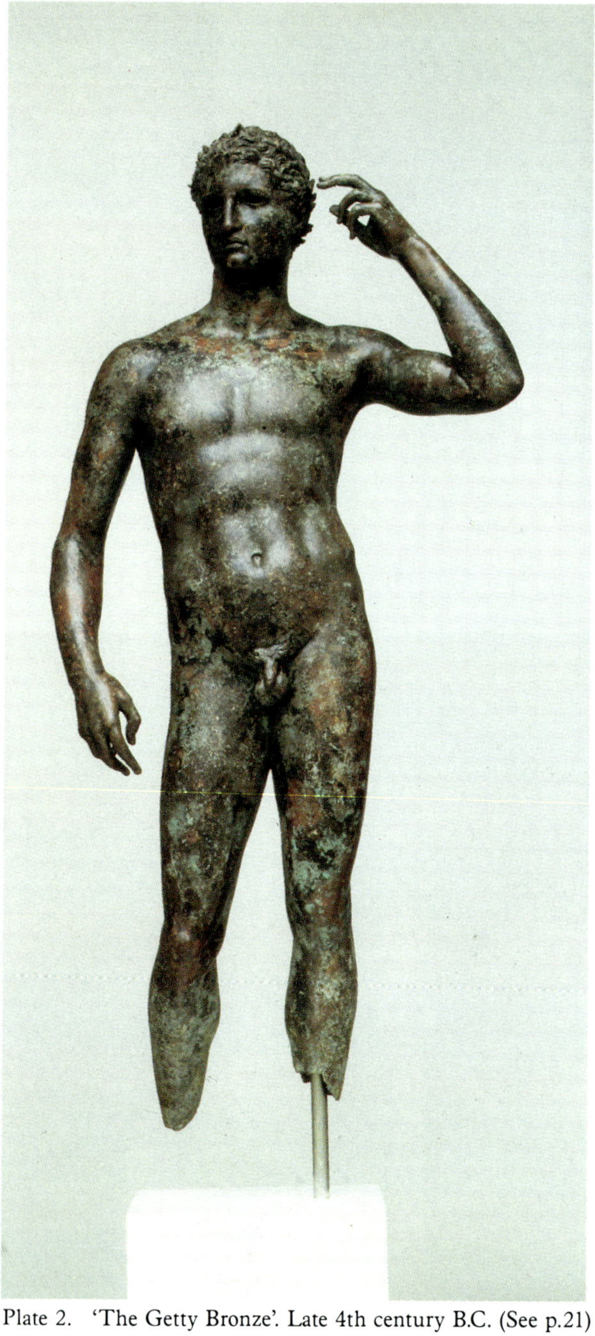

Plate 2. 'The Getty Bronze'. Late 4th century B.C. (See p.21)

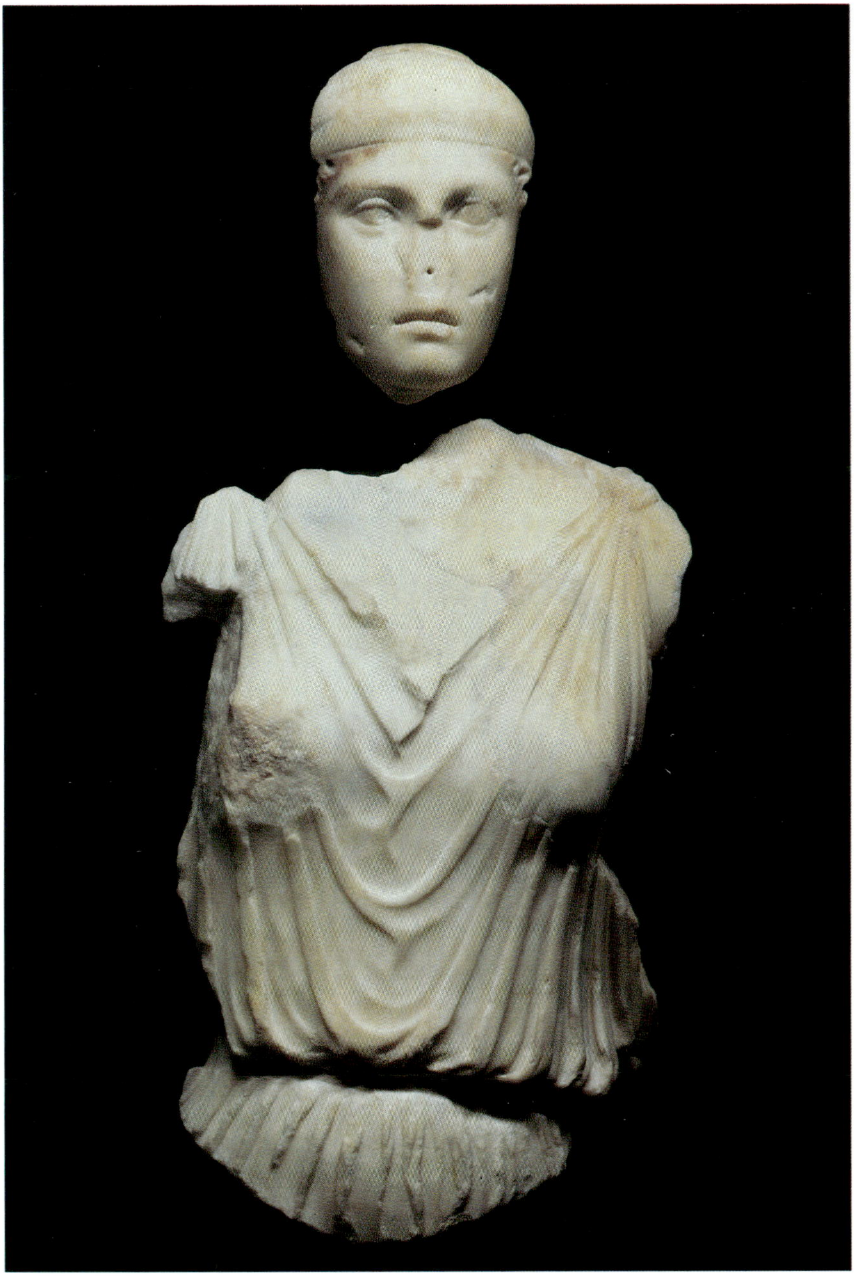

Plate 3. Nike or Amazon, from the Apollo Sosianus temple, Rome. Ca. 430 B.C.
(See p.33)

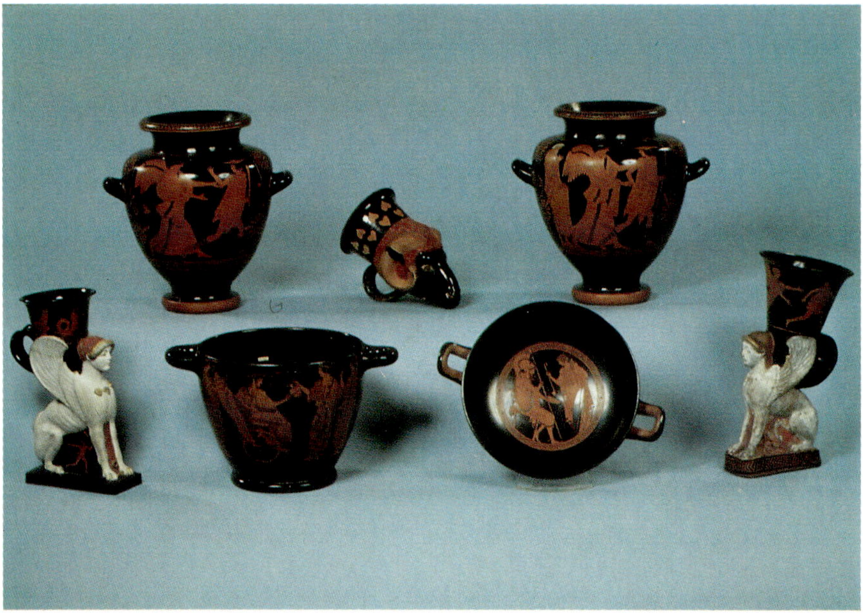

Plate 4A. The vases from the Brygos Tomb, near Capua. Ca. 490-460 B.C. (See p.42)

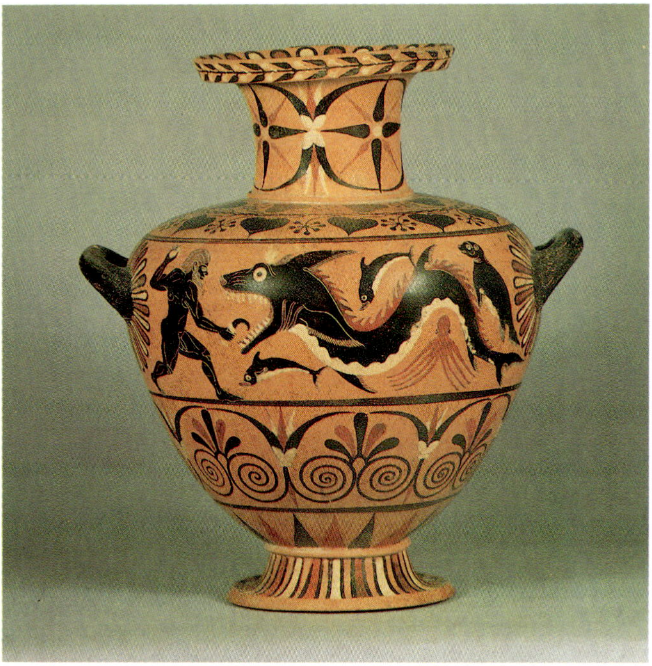

Plate 4B. Herakles fights a sea monster. Caeretan hydria. Ca. 530-520 B.C. (See p.44)

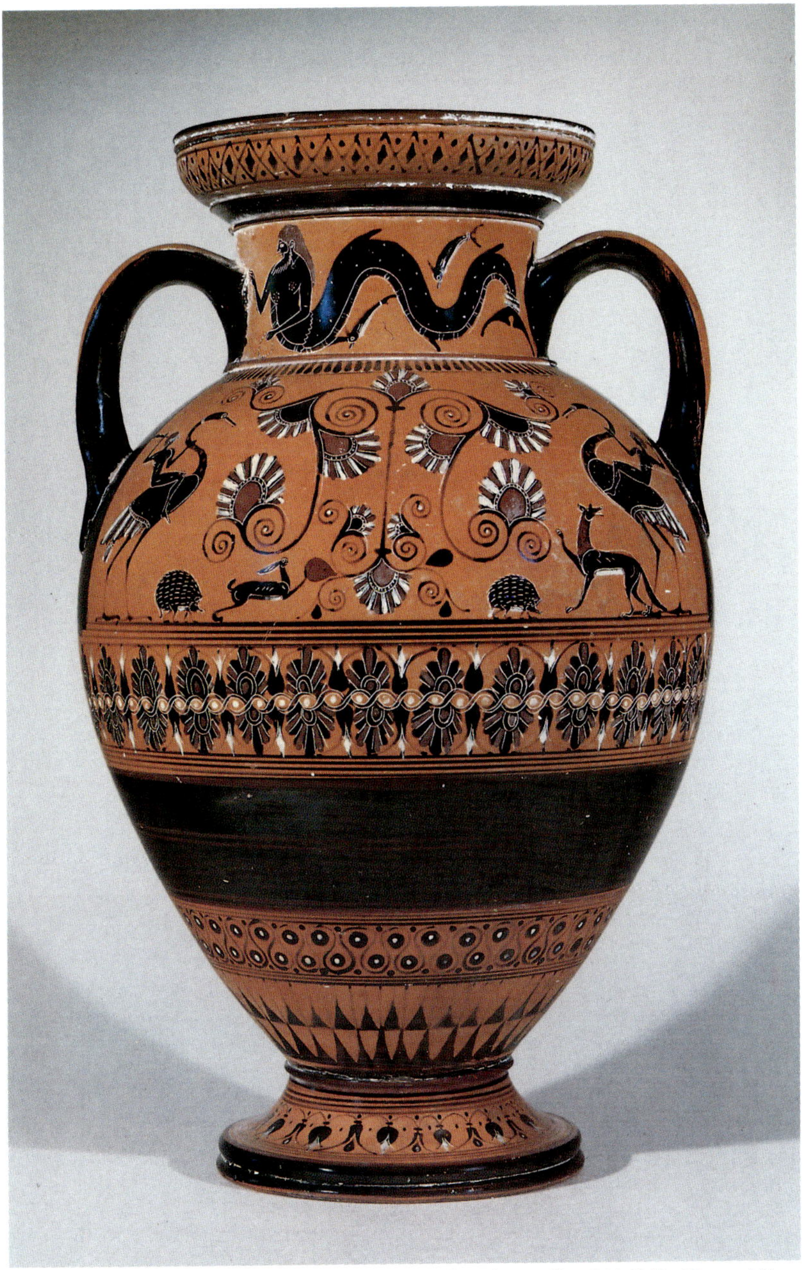

Plate 5. 'Floral fantasy'. The Northampton Amphora. Ca. 540 B.C. (See p.44)

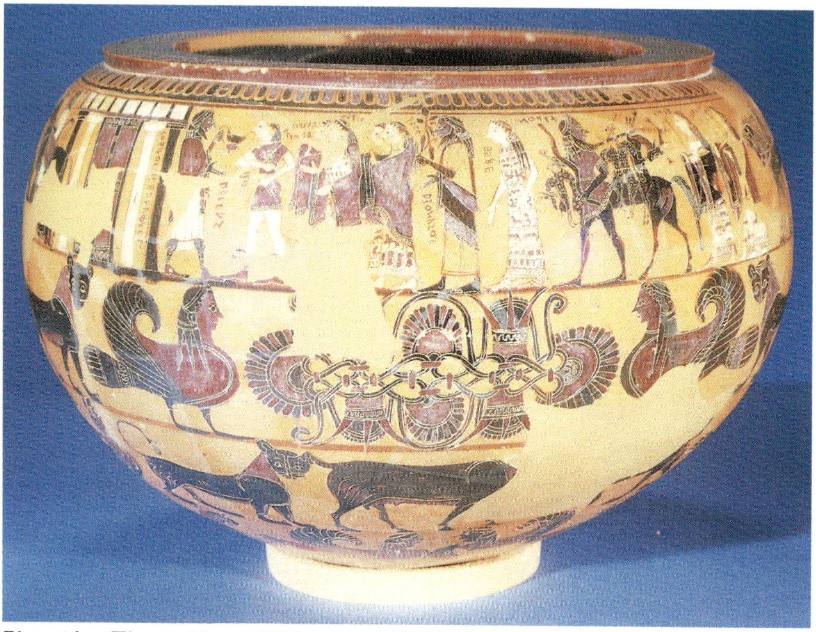

Plate 6A. The wedding of Peleus and Thetis. Attic black-figure dinos, signed by Sophilos. Ca. 580 B.C. (See p.45)

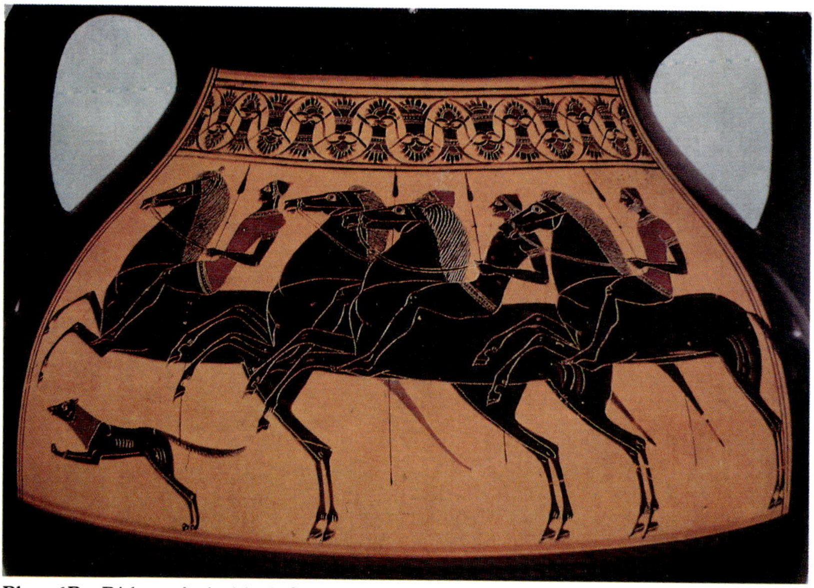

Plate 6B Riders. Attic black-figure amphora, attributed to the Amasis Painter. Ca. 540 B.C. (See p.46)

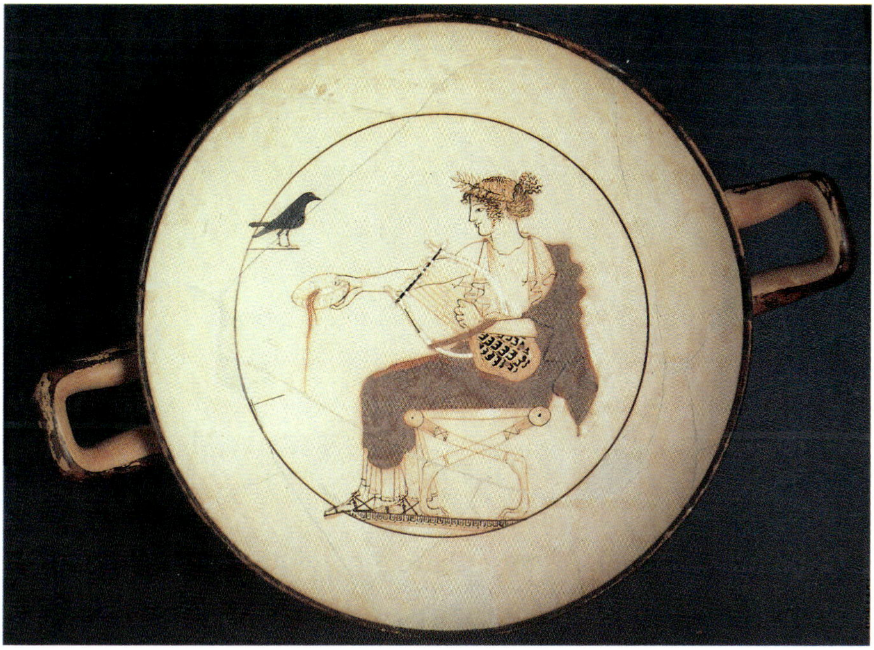

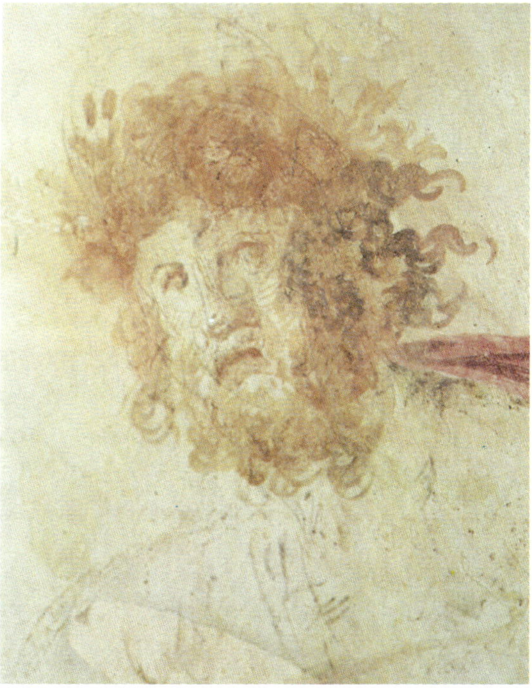

Plate 7A. Seated Apollo. Attic white-ground cup, from Delphi. Ca. 470 B.C. (See p.47)

Plate 7B. Head of Hades, from wall-painting in tomb at Vergina. Ca. 350 B.C. (See p.49)

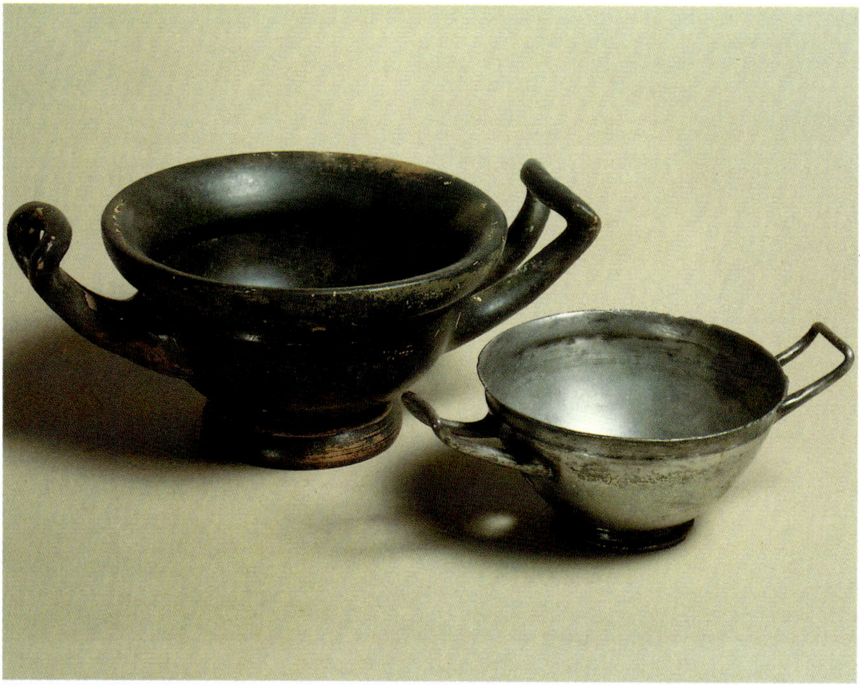

Plate 8A. Silver and clay cup-skyphoi. Early 4th century B.C. (See p.59)

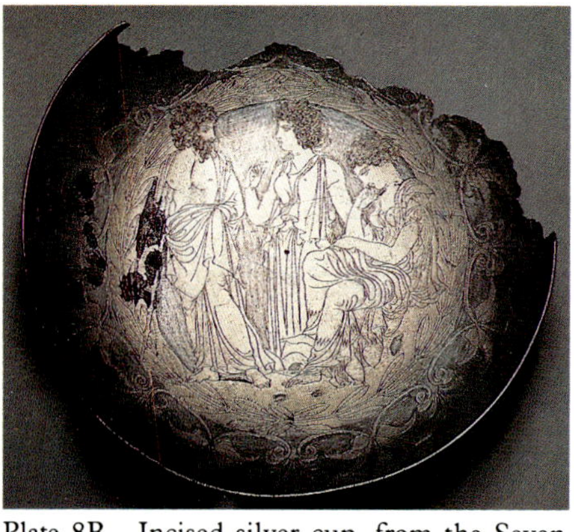

Plate 8B. Incised silver cup, from the Seven Brothers barrows. 450-425 B.C. (See p.59)

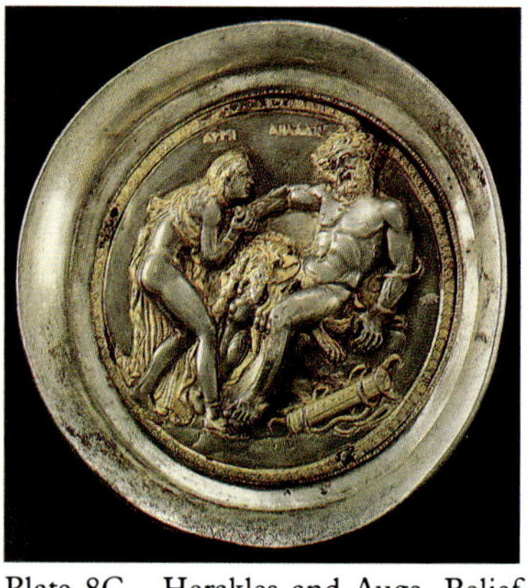

Plate 8C. Herakles and Auge. Relief silver cup from the Rogozen hoard. Early 4th century B.C. (See p.59)

It is now agreed that because of their size 'Mausolus' and 'Artemisia' did not stand in the chariot on the top of the pyramid; one of the occupants may have been Mausolus or perhaps Apollo. The two figures that have survived must be for us nameless ancestors of the royal house, but the portrait-like features of 'Mausolus' nonetheless show the importance of work on the periphery of the Greek world for the history of Greek portraiture.[48] The tiny portrait heads (e.g. Colour Plate 1B) found in the tomb of Philip II at Vergina[49] are part of the same development and lead on to the portraits, both royal and other, that are one of the main characteristics of the Hellenistic period.[50]

Indeed, the whole temple-tomb of the Mausoleum itself points forward not only to the greater importance of the individual but also to the notion of spectacular display and erudition in non-civic and non-religious contexts. The final flourish of this approach can be seen in the spectacular finds from Sperlonga, the grotto of Tiberius' villa near Formiae.[51] The cave was designed to accommodate a round and rectangular pool, the latter with a dining room placed in the centre. The sculptural groups were set at the edges and in the middle of the round pool. At the back of the cave was the largest of all the groups, that of the blinding of the Cyclops (Fig. 19), with the giant lying back and the Greek heroes crowding round him. In the middle of the round pool stood the slightly smaller but much more complicated group of Skylla wrecking Odysseus' ship. It is on the carving of the boat that the names of the artists are found: 'Athanodoros/ Hagesandros's son/ and/ Hagesandros/ Paionios' son/ and Polydoros/ Polydoros' son/ Rhodians made (the work)', names which Pliny (36.37)

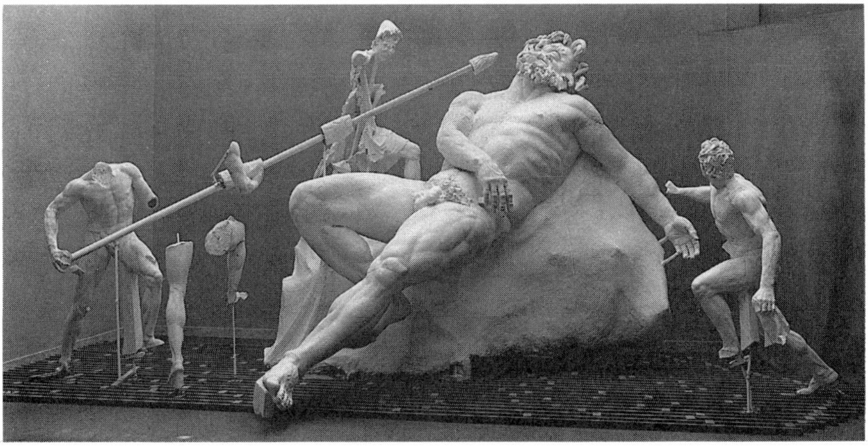

19. The Cyclops group, from Sperlonga. First century A.D.

gives as the sculptors of the original group of the Laocoon. Two smaller groups of two figures each were set close to the rectangular pool. These also concerned Odysseus, one a version of the theft of the Palladion by Odysseus and Diomedes, the other a version of the 'Pasquino' but not this time Melenaus dragging the body of Patroklos but rather (because of a curious treatment of the lower leg of the dead figure) Odysseus dragging Achilles' body from the battlefield, his Achilles' heel made prominent. The whole programme seems to have been designed to glorify the hero Odysseus, and it would be good to know which emperor saw himself in such a role. The date of the ensemble has been seen to be Tiberian or even as late as Flavian. It is a bravura performance that feeds on the seemingly inexhaustible fund of Greek heroic legend and on the Greek sculptors' technical virtuosity.

NOTES

1. See II, n. 5, p. 183.

2. J. L. Benson, 'The central group of the Corfu pediment', *Gestalt und Geschichte. Festschrift Karl Schefold zu seinem sechzigsten Geburtstag am 26 Januar 1965*, ed. M. Rohde-Liegle, H. A. Cahn and H. Chr. Ackermann (*AK* Beiheft 4, 1967), pp. 48–60, pl. 15 (quotation from 60); J. M. Hemelrijk, *Gnomon* 42 (1970), 169–70; Robertson *HGA*, pp. 63–7 and *SHGA*, pp. 16–17.

3. J. Boardman *GSAP*, pp. 153–4. For Herakles and Peisistratos, see pp. 70–1.

4. J. Boardman, 'Herakles, Theseus and Amazons', *Eye of Greece*, pp. 1–16, pls. 1–6. For a new reconstruction of the metopes, see K. Hoffelner, 'Die Metopen des Athena-Schatzhauses: ein neuer Rekonstruktionsversuch', *AM* 103 (1988), 77–117, Beil. 5. The evidence of Pausanias: 10.11.4. For the Siphnian Treasure, see pp. 3–6.

5. Full publication: E. Touloupa, *Τὰ ἐναέτια γλυπτά τοῦ ναοῦ τοῦ 'Απόλλωνος Δαφνηφόρου στήν 'Ερέτρια* (Ioannina, 1983). See also E. Touloupa, 'Die Giebelskulpturen des Apollon Daphnephorostempels in Eretria', *AKGP* I, pp. 143–51, pls. 59–65, Beil. 2; and Boardman, *Eye of Greece*, pp. 8–9. J. Frel, 'Notes on some archaic Attic sculpture', *GettyMJ* 10 (1982), 95–104, esp. 98 connects other work with the 'master' of the pediment. For the Apollo Sosianus temple, see pp. 33–4.

6. D. Ohly, *Die Aegineten* I, *Die Ostgiebelgruppe* (Munich, 1976); D. Williams, 'Aigina, Aphaia-Tempel XI: the pottery from the second limestone temple and the later history of the sanctuary', *AA* 1987, 629–680 and D. W. J. Gill, 'The temple of Aphaia on Aegina: the date of the reconstruction', *BSA* 83 (1988), 169–77 (bringing the date down below 480 B.C.).

7. B. Ashmole, N. Yalouris and A. Frantz, *Olympia, the Sculptures of the Temple of Zeus* (London, 1967).

8. J. Barron, 'Bakchylides, Theseus and a woolly cloak', *BICS* 27 (1980), 1–8 and 'Alkamenes at Olympia', *BICS* 31 (1984), 199–211, pls. 10–12.

9. For a recent history of the Akropolis, see U. Muss and Ch. Schubert, *Die Akropolis von Athen* (Graz, 1988).

10. On preserving the monuments, see *2nd International Meeting for the Restoration of the Acropolis Monuments, Parthenon, Athens 12–14 September 1983, Proceedings* (Athens, 1985); *The Acropolis at Athens, Conservation, Restoration and Research 1975–1983*, Ministry of Culture, Committee for the Preservation of the Acropolis Monuments (1986); E. Touloupa, 'On preserving the monuments of the Athenian Acropolis', *AJA* 91 (1987), 306–7.

11. B. F. Cook, *The Elgin Marbles* (London, 1984); C. Hitchins, *The Elgin Marbles: should they be returned to Greece?* (London, 1987). A useful introduction to the Parthenon: S. Woodford, *The Parthenon* (Cambridge, 1981).

12. A. Mantis, 'Akropolis 2381', *BCH* 110 (1986), 231–5 and 'Un nouveau fragment de la 10e métope sud du Parthenon', 619–24; 'Neue Fragmente von Parthenonskulpturen', *AKGP* II, pp. 71–6, pls. 102–6; 'Contribution à la reconstruction de la 11e métope sud du Parthenon', *BCH* 111 (1987), 137–46; 'Neue Fragmente von Parthenon-Metopen', *JDAI* 102 (1987), 163–84; 'Beiträge zur Wiederherstellung der mittleren Südmetopen des Parthenon', *Himmelmann Festschrift*, pp. 109–14, pls. 18–19. See also G. Despinis, *Parthenoneia* (Athens, 1982) and 'Neue Fragmente von Parthenonskulpturen und Bemerkungen zur Rekonstruktion des Parthenon-Ostgiebels', *Parthenon-Kongress*, pp. 293–302, pls. 36–46.

13. For the work in the Antikenmuseum, Basel, see E. Berger's articles in *AK* 19 (1976), 122–42; 20 (1977), 124–41; 23 (1980), 56–100; 24 (1981), 98–102; 25 (1982), 162–8; 26 (1983), 110–3; *Die Geburt der Athena im Ostgiebel des Parthenon* (Basel, 1974); and a most important volume, *Der Parthenon in Basel, Dokumentation zu den Metopen* (Mainz, 1986), based on the study of casts in Basel (other volumes will follow).

14. *Parthenon-Kongress* – an important work of reference.

15. F. Brommer, *Die Skulpturen der Parthenon-Giebel* (Mainz, 1963), *Die Metopen der Parthenon* (Mainz, 1967) and *Der Parthenonfries* (Mainz, 1977). These are being updated by Berger's documentation, see n. 13 above. See also Brommer's general survey, *The Sculptures of the Parthenon: metopes, frieze, pediments, cult-statue,* trans. M. Whittall (London, 1979) and compare J. Boardman and D. Finn, *The Parthenon and its Sculptures* (London, 1985).

16. R. Carpenter, *The Architects of the Parthenon* (Harmondsworth, 1970); H. Drerup, 'Parthenon und Vorparthenon – zum Stand der Kontroverse', *AK* 24 (1981), 21–38, pls. 4–5; and see Berger's book on the metopes (n. 13 above).

17. West: B. Wesenberg, 'Perser oder Amazonen', *AA* 1983, 203–8. East: M. A. Tiverios, 'Observations on the East metopes of the Parthenon', *AJA* 86 (1982), 227–9, pl. 29.

18. North: J. Dörig, 'Les Métopes nord du Parthénon', *Parthenon-Kongress,* pp. 202–5, pl. 15, 1. South: E. Simon, 'Versuch einer Deutung der Südmetopen des Parthenon', *JDAI* 90 (1975), 100–20; M. Robertson, 'Two question marks on the Parthenon', *Blanckenhagen Festschrift*, pp. 75–87, esp. 78–87 (quotation from 78) and 'The south metopes: Theseus and Daidalos', *Parthenon-Kongress,* pp. 206–9, pls. 15.2–16. See also B. Wesenberg, 'Parthenongebälk und Südmetopenproblem', *JDAI* 98 (1983), 57–86. For examples of the influence of the metopes on vase-paintings, see recently K.A. Schwab, 'A Parthenonian centaur', *Greek Vases* II (1985), pp. 89–94 and 'The gods of the Parthenon north metopes N31 and N32', *AJA* 90 (1986), 207. See also n. 12 above.

19. E. Simon, 'Die Mittelgruppe im Westgiebel des Parthenon', *Tainia*, pp. 239–55, pls. 51–4. A reclaimed head: M. Bruskari, 'Die Wiedergewinnung eines Kopfes aus dem Westgiebel des Parthenons', *AK* 30 (1987), 119–22, pl. 17. See also K. Arafat, *Classical Zeus*, (Oxford, 1990), pp. 156–9.

20. See nn. 13 and 14.

21. B. B. Shefton, 'The krater from Baksy', *Eye of Greece*, pp. 149–81, pls. 41–8. See also p. 17.

22. M. Robertson and A. Frantz, *The Parthenon Frieze* (London,1975).

23. J. Boardman, 'The Parthenon frieze – another view', *Brommer Festschrift*, pp. 39–49, pl. 16; and 'The Parthenon frieze', *Parthenon-Kongress*, pp. 210–15.

24. E.g. A. Linfert, 'Die Götterversammlung im Parthenon-Ostfries und das attische Kultsystem unter Perikles', *AM* 94 (1979), 41–7; E. Simon, 'Die Mittelszene im Ostfries des Parthenon', *AM* 97 (1982), 127–44, pls. 23–8; I. S. Mark, 'The Gods on the East frieze of the Parthenon', *Hesperia* 53 (1984), 289–342, pls. 61–6; I. D. Jenkins, 'The composition of the so-called Eponymous Heroes on the East frieze of the Parthenon', *AJA* 89 (1985), 121–7; L. Beschi, '*Η ζωφόρος του Παρθενώνα – μία νέα προτάση ερμηνείας*', *AKGP* II, pp. 199–224; T. Schäfer, 'Diphroi und Peplos auf dem Ostfries des Parthenon: zur Kultpraxis bei den Panathenäen in klassischer Zeit', *AM* 102 (1987), 185–212, pl. 14; J. Boardman, 'Notes on the Parthenon East frieze', *Kanon*, pp. 9–14, pls. 4–6; C. Clairmont, 'Girl or boy? Parthenon East frieze 35', *AA* 1989, 495–6. See also articles in the *Parthenon-Kongress* volume.

25. F. Brommer, *Die Parthenonfries* (Mainz, 1977), pp. 168–70.

26. 'The viewing and the obscuring of the Parthenon frieze', *JHS* 107 (1987), 98–105, pls. 1–2a (quotation from 104). Cf. R. Stillwell, 'The Panathenaic frieze', *Hesperia* 38 (1969), 231–41, pls. 61–3. Osborne (105) doubts the identity of Parthenon frieze workmen and carvers of late

fifth-century grave stelai, pointing out that style is not the only criterion, 'shared visual ideology' must also be taken into account. For a recent history of grave reliefs, see B. Schmaltz, *Griechische Grabreliefs* (Darmstadt, 1983).

27. N. Leipen, *Athena Parthenos, a Reconstruction* (Toronto, 1971) and 'Athena Parthenos: problems of reconstruction', *Parthenon-Kongress*, pp. 177–81, pls. 6–9; A. J. N. W. Prag, 'Athena Mancuniensis: another copy of the Athena Parthenos', *JHS* 92 (1972), 96–114, pls. 19–23 and 'New copies of the Athena Parthenos from the East', *Parthenon-Kongress*, pp. 182–7, pls. 10–12; P. Karanastassis, 'Untersuchungen zur kaiserzeitlichen Plastik in Griechenland II: Kopien, Varianten und Umbildungen nach Athena-Typen des 5. Jhs v. Chr. A. Athena-Parthenos', *AM* 102 (1987), 323–428, pls. 35–57.

28. Shield: E. B. Harrison, 'Motifs of the City-siege on the shield of Athena Parthenos', *AJA* 85 (1981), 281–317, pls. 46–54; V. M. Strocka, 'Das Schildrelief – Zum Stand der Forschung', *Parthenon-Kongress*, pp. 188–96, pl. 13; K. W. Arafat, 'A note on the Athena Parthenos', *BSA* 81 (1986), 1–6; D. Mauruschat, 'Ein neuer Vorschlag zur Rekonstruktion der Schildamazonomachie der Athena Parthenos', *Boreas* 10 (1987), 32–58; H. Meyer, 'Ein neues Piräusreliefs. Zur Überlieferung der Amazonomachie am Schild der Athena-Parthenos', *AM* 102 (1987), 295–321, pls. 29–34; W. Gauer, 'Parthenonische Amazonomachie und Perserkrieg', *Kanon*, pp. 28–41. For the mistaken Pheidias-Daidalos connection with the shield, see F. Preisshofen, 'Phidias-Daedalus auf dem Schild der Athena-Parthenos? Ampelius 8,10', *JDAI* 89 (1974), 50–69.

29. A. W. Lawrence, 'The Acropolis and Persepolis', *JHS* 71 (1951), 111–19.

30. M. C. Root, 'The Parthenon frieze and the Apadana reliefs at Persepolis: reassessing a programmatic relationship', *AJA* 89 (1985), 103–20, pls. A, 22–25 (quotation from 120). See also her *The King and Kingship in Achaemenid Art: essays on the creation of an iconography of empire* (Leiden, 1979).

31. Ares temple: E. B. Harrison 'The classical high-relief frieze from the Athenian Agora', *AKGP* II, pp. 109–17, pls. 117–22 (doesn't belong to the temple); Poseidon temple, Sounion: F. Felten and K. Hoffelner, 'Die Relieffriese des Poseidontempels in Sunion', *AM* 102 (1987), 169–84, Beil. 1–2; Nemesis temple, Rhamnous: M. M. Miles, 'A reconstruction of the temple of Nemesis at Rhamnous', *Hesperia* 58 (1989), 131–249, pls. 29–48, and see p. 18 above for the cult statue and base.

32. Hephaisteion: S. von Bockelberg, *AntPl* 18 (Berlin, 1979), 23–50, pls. 10–48 (430–425 B.C.). E. B. Harrison denies that the temple is the Hephaisteion and names it the temple of Artemis Eukleia, *AJA* 81 (1977), 139, n. 14.

33. J. Dörig, *La frise est de l'Héphaisteion* (Mainz, 1985).

34. Erekhtheion: P. N. Boulter, *AntPl* 10 (Berlin, 1970) (frieze); E. E. Schmidt, *AntPl* 13 (Berlin, 1973) (copies of the Caryatids); H. Lauter, *AntPl* 16 (Berlin, 1976) (the Caryatids); M. Brouskari, '*ΖΩΙΔΙΑ ΛΑΙΝΕΑ*. Nouvelles figures de la frise de l'Erechtheion', *Kanon*, pp. 60–8, pls. 15–16.

35. K. Jeppesen, *The Theory of the Alternative Erechtheion* (Aarhus, 1987).

36. Nike temple: H. B. Mattingly, 'The Athena Nike temple reconsidered', *AJA* 86 (1982), 381–5 (late 420s B.C.). See also E. Simon, 'Zur Sandalenlöserin der Nikebalustrade', *Kanon*, pp. 69–73, pls. 20–21 on the balustrade. Ilissos temple: C. A. Picon, 'The Ilissos temple reconsidered', *AJA* 82 (1978), 47–81 (425–420 B.C.); A. Krug, *AntPl* 18 (Berlin, 1979), 7–21, pls. 1–9; M. M. Miles, 'The date of the temple on the Ilissus River', *Hesperia* 49 (1980), 309–25, pls. 91–6 (435–430 B.C.); W. A. P. Childs, 'In defense of an early date for the frieze of the temple on the Ilissus', *AM* 100 (1985), 207–51, pls. 43–5 (440s).

37. E. B. Harrison, *AJA* 85 (1981), 233.

38. S. B. Platner and T. Ashby, *A Topographical Dictionary of Ancient Rome* (Oxford, 1929), pp. 15–16; E. Nash, *A Pictorial Dictionary of Ancient Rome* I (London, 1961), pp. 28–9.

39. E. La Rocca, *Amazzonomachia, Le sculture frontonali del tempio di Apollo Sosiano* (Rome, 1985); 'Le sculture frontonali del tempio di Apollo Sosiano a Roma', *AKGP* II, pp. 51–58, pls. 95–9, Beil. 3. See now R. M. Cook, 'The Pediment of Apollo Sosianus', *AA* 1989, 525–8, for a different arrangement of the fifth-century compositon.

40. For Theseus, see Boardman *GSCP* fig. 134; for the kneeling Amazon from the earlier pediment, see Boardman *GSAP* fig. 205.1.

41. See p. 7.

42. For the Niobid figures, see Boardman *GSCP* fig. 133.1–3. For the Niobids in art, see R. M. Cook, *Niobe and her children* (Cambridge, 1964). For Greek art in Rome, see J. J. Pollitt, 'The impact of Greek art on Rome', *TAPA* 108 (1978), 155–74.

43. For the latest statement, see N. Yalouris, 'Die Skulpturen des Asklepiostempels von Epidauros', *AKGP* II, pp. 175–84, pls. 148–53, Beil. 4. This volume has much more on other fourth-century architectural sculpture. See also B. R. Brown, *Anticlassicism in Greek sculpture of the fourth century B.C.* (New York, 1973) for new trends. For Skopas and Tegea, see p. 20.

44. Bassai: F. R. Cooper, *The temple of Apollo at Bassai* (University Microfilms, Ann Arbor, 1971); C. Hofkes-Brukker, *Der Bassai-Fries* (Munich, 1975); N. Yalouris, 'Problems relating to the temple of Apollo Epikourios at Bassai', *Acta of the XI International Congress of Classical Archaeology* (London, 1979), pp. 89–104, pls. 37–46; C. A. Picon, 'The Orpheus metope from Bassai', *BSA* 76 (1981), 323–8, pl. 56.

45. J. C. Carter, *The Sculpture of the temple of Athena Polias at Priene* (London, 1983).

46. Reports of the Danish Archaeological Expedition to Bodrum are beginning to appear, published by Aarhus University Press: 1. *The Sacrificial Deposit* (1981); 2. *The Written Sources and the Archaeological Background* (1986). To come are; 3. *The Maussolleion Terrace and Accessory Structures* and 4. *The Sepulchral Monument: Site, Foundation, Tomb Chamber and Superstructure*. See also S. Hornblower, *Mausolus* (Oxford, 1982), ch. IX.

47. G. B. Waywell, *The Freestanding Sculptures of the Mausoleum at Halicarnassus in the British Museum: a Catalogue* (London, 1978). For sorting out some of the frieze blocks and fragments, see B. Ashmole, 'A new join in the Amazon frieze of the Mausoleum', *JHS* 89 (1969), 22–3, pl. 1, and B. F. Cook, 'The Mausoleum frieze: membra disjectanda', *BSA* 71 (1976), 49–54, pls. 6–7.

48. Robertson *HGA*, pp. 457–8; *SHGA*, pp. 184–5.

49. M. Andronikos, 'The tombs at the Great Tumulus of Vergina', *Acta of the XI International Congress of Classical Archaeology* (London, 1979), pp. 39–56, pls. 1–30; *Vergina* (Athens, 1984), pp. 123–6, and many other publications. For the relation of the miniature ivory head to the skull, see A. J. N. W. Prag, J. H. Musgrave and R. A. H. Neave, 'The skull from Tomb II at Vergina: King Philip II of Macedon', *JHS* 104 (1984), 60–78, pls. 2–7, and A. J. N. W. Prag, 'Reconstructing King Philip II: the "nice" version', *AJA* 94 (1990), 237–47.

50. J. J. Pollitt, *Art in the Hellenistic Age* (Cambridge, 1986), chs. 1 and 3, and R. R. R. Smith, *Hellenistic Royal Portraits* (Oxford, 1988).

51. G. Säflund, *The Polyphemos and Scylla Groups at Sperlonga* (Stockholm, 1972); B. Conticello and B. Andreae, *AntPl* 14 (Berlin, 1974); A. F. Stewart, 'To entertain an emperor: Sperlonga. Laokoon and Tiberius at the dinner-table', *JRS* 67 (1977), 76–90, pls. 9–12; B. Andreae and B. Conticello, *Skylla und Charybdis. Zur Skylla-Gruppe von Sperlonga* (Stuttgart, 1987); R. Neudecker, *Die Skulpturen-Ausstattung römischer Villen in Italien* (Mainz, 1988), no. 62, Beil. 3. For the Laocoon and Sperlonga sculptures, see G. Daltrop, *Die Laokoongruppe im Vatikan* (Constanz, 1982); B. Andreae, *Laokoon und die Gründung Roms* (Mainz, 1988) and S. Howard, 'Laokoon rerestored', *AJA* 93 (1989), 417–22.

IV. CONNOISSEURSHIP

In the summer of 1985 the centenary of the birth of Sir John Beazley was celebrated in London and Oxford.[1] His influence on the study of Greek painted pottery, particularly Attic (Colour Plate 4A, etc.), has been second to none this century, and his death in 1970 left a gap that has been impossible to fill. Since his death, titles of lectures and conferences such as 'Beazley and After', 'Vasenforschung nach Beazley' and 'In the Wake of Beazley' show what a pivotal figure he was, and the 70s and 80s have proved interesting times for re-adjusting sights. As Martin Robertson remarked, we are living in 'an age of uncertainty.[2]

Mention should be made here of the Beazley archive – the magnificent collection of photographs and of his own drawings that Beazley bequeathed to the Ashmolean Museum in Oxford.[3] The photographic archive is being increased annually, and the published references that Beazley meticulously logged are being kept up to date on computer with occasional publications of the lists of newly-published pictures of the vases that Beazley attributed.[4] Record is also being kept of the vases that have come to light since the late 60s when Beazley stopped collecting references, and lists of those are promised. Other publications updating Beazley's work are mentioned below.

Beazley's achievement was colossal, and his approach not only set Attic black- and red-figure vase-painting on a surer footing but also affected the attitude of scholars to the other vase-painting, both earlier and later. The method he adopted was not new but had never been carried to such lengths; it was not only the 'unconscious' details of a man's work that claimed his attention, he considered every aspect of the finished product. A meticulous study of line and composition recreated personalities from the Athenian pottery workshops and showed their relationships to one another; indeed, he freed the study from rigid compartmentalization and made the painting of Greek pottery a supple, living tradition. The method needs a keen eye, a retentive memory and a sensitive understanding of artistic style, together with a vast knowledge of Classical literature and a chalcenteric application to work, and these were united in Beazley. He rarely explained his method, but recently Donna Kurtz, the keeper of the Beazley Archive, has collected and elaborated on Beazley's brief comments on his approach.[5]

Many years ago Martin Robertson dubbed Greek vase-painting 'a very curious phenomenon'[6] – it combines the craft of the potter with the art of draughtsmanship in a unique way. More recently in coming to grips with the post-Beazleyan world, he has seen two major problems. He accepts that the major figures that Beazley isolated – the Berlin Painter, the Kleophrades Painter, the Achilles Painter, etc. – are well established, he sees the difficulties to lie in the minor figures and in their individual identity and relationship to one another and to the major figures.[7] A second point he makes is that whilst Beazley must be congratulated for applying his method to all painters, no matter what quality (Robertson's phrase is that 'there is no place to get a knife in'), this overall approach has tended to mask the difference between art and hack work. 'Potters were there primarily to provide cheap household ware for a wide public, and the bulk of Attic black-figure and red-figure is just that, and has little or nothing to do with fine art.' Thus the method of work is applicable to any vase-painting, but distinctions of quality need to be kept in mind, as Beazley did indeed do. Robertson also warns against an excessive reverence for, and an overeager rejection of, Beazley's methods and results. 'This has led some people to accept Beazley's attributions as a matter of faith, others to dismiss the whole thing as something of a confidence-trick; both, surely, mistaken attitudes.'[8]

Many scholars and students continue to work within Beazley's framework of stylistic analysis. Some choose to look more closely at the painters he defined, incorporating new work and charting the development of individual styles; others reshuffle his lists, merging and separating the pieces; some apply his methods to new areas beyond any that he himself studied. The approach has become part of the basic way of looking at Greek painted pottery, as it enables us to see how the Greek artists represented the world around them, what a particular generation of painters contributed to the development of their craft, how an individual personality developed, what were the different subjects that interested artists, and also what they teach us of the lost panel paintings that our written sources praise so highly.[9]

Geometric and Archaic

The method is now well established in the study of Geometric pottery,[10] particularly at the time when figured and narrative scenes are coming into being. To make headway, there is need for sufficient diagnostic detail, whether of patterns or figures, and for sufficient material. Recent work on Corinthian vase-painting, from Late Geometric to the sixth century, shows the difficulties encountered when dealing with a limited body of evidence. Benson now shies away from 'painters' and 'masters' and prefers to speak more warily of 'workshops' and 'groups', and comparison of his lists with those of Amyx where they overlap shows that there is still wide room for individual disagreement.[11] Amyx's work is not only confined to connoisseurship, and his book is now a basic tool for any further work on the archaic pottery of Corinth. Athens in the seventh century was not a large producer of painted pottery, and the question has recently been raised of whether some of the Protoattic pottery that we usually connect with Athens (the 'Black and White' style of such pieces as the Polyphemos amphora in Eleusis; and the work of the Ram Jug Painter and the New York Nessos Painter) may not perhaps have been eccentric to the Attic tradition and made on the nearby island of Aegina where some have been found.[12] The later development of Athens as a prolific centre of fine pottery production should not necessarily be reflected back to an earlier century.

Other centres of pottery production in the Archaic period besides Athens and Corinth lend themselves with varied success, both in results and in importance, to the distinguishing of individual painters. The Cyclades and the Asia Minor seaboard and its adjacent islands are still problem areas. The Northampton amphora (Colour Plate 5) is a prime example of the difficulties some of the centres pose. The style is East Greek, but the group of which it is the name-piece, has been assigned to various centres in Ionia, to Samos, to the Cyclades, and to Etruria. The last location would make it an example of work done by immigrant Ionian artists.[13] The editors of a new series of volumes under the general title of 'Kerameus', which for the Attic black- and red-figure techniques concentrates on single painters (see below), have issued two volumes on non-Attic work of the sixth century: one on the painters of Klazomenian sarcophagi[14] at work in Klazomenai between 530 and 450 B.C., and one on the vastly entertaining painters of Caeretan hydriai (Colour Plate 4B)[15] who moved from East Greece to Italy (via Egypt?) and worked at Caere from 530 to 500 B.C. The scale of the publications and the generous number of illustrations mean that the style of each painter can be studied closely and the bases for attribution individually tested; and both authors consider, when appropriate, aspects such as distribution and burial practices. Laconian also has now been mapped in this way,[16] and mention might be made of Nigel Spivey's study of the Etruscan Micali Painter and his followers, working in Vulci in the late sixth century.[17] The Micali Painter's flamboyant figures, who, as Spivey so engagingly says, 'do not customarily loiter or pose, but rather rush, flap, and jive their way around the pot', are good examples of what others did with more sober Attic compositions and also how a minor figure from an artistic point of view can be shown to be an interesting figure whom one is happy to get to know more closely – he is, in

Spivey's words, the only painter who 'could choreograph a can-can for a centaur'.

Attic Black-figure

Not surprisingly, the major work of connoisseurship has been carried out in Attic black- and red-figure and in South Italian. Boardman took advantage of the Beazley Archive and produced in quick succession his handbooks on Attic black-figure[18] and archaic red-figure,[19] and has recently followed them up with a classical red-figure volume.[20] These three handbooks treat the development of vase-painting over three centuries by concentrating on the major, and some minor, artists. The thumbnail sketches of the careers of the various painters and their grouping together in workshops and groups present a lively picture of the different potters' shops.

Some of Beazley's published works on Attic black-figure have been reissued. His Sather series of lectures on the development of Attic black-figure[21] has been published in a new edition with some updating, and his much earlier sketch of Attic black-figure is now included in a volume of his individual lectures.[22] As mentioned above, new publications of attributed vases are listed in the *Beazley Addenda* volumes.[23]

There has been much recent work on the individual painters in black-figure in Athens. A full-scale study of Sophilos by Bakir,[24] with excellent photographic coverage, discards some of Beazley's attributions and even denies the role of potter to Sophilos. The Erskine dinos in the British Museum (Colour Plate 6A) shows the strengths and weaknesses of the artist, and Dyfri Williams in his detailed monograph on the vase[25] elucidates the arrangement of the Peleus and Thetis procession and the various groups of deities and subordinates, and suggests that the vase was made as a wedding present. The same has been suggested for the François Vase painted by Kleitias which shares the same theme, and Andrew Stewart would link the scenes with Stesichoros.[26] The François Vase has had more adventures in modern times than most others, and an Italian monograph on the history of the vase (it was discovered in 1846) not only charts its physical history but also shows how early its quality was appreciated, at a time when little was known about the history of vase-painting and scant attention paid to black-figure.[27]

Lydos has also received a full treatment,[28] and the painters of the old-fashioned Tyrrhenian amphorae continue to attract more attention than they perhaps deserve: how late do they date, were they made in Athens or further north or maybe as far as Eretria, what is their connection with their Etruscan counterparts in shape?[29] Cup-painters are being studied by Brijder[30] who claims that the shapes of the Komast and Siana cup were of Athenian origin and originated at much the same time, both new and dubious ideas. He also reshuffles many of Beazley's attributions without explanation and on occasion confuses potter and painter. Exekias needs a new volume;[31] his work would fit well into the 'Kerameus' series which has already issued treatments of the Affecter[32] and the Swing Painter.[33] The Amasis Painter is the black-figure artist who has received the most favoured attention. His work was chosen for a commemorative exhibition in New York, timed to coincide with the centenary of Beazley's birth, and a detailed and beautifully illustrated, if somewhat dauntingly academic, catalogue shows the wealth of information that can be won from a close study of a single painter. New works by the Amasis Painter enlarge his repertoire, as for instance the horsemen on the Munich amphora (Colour Plate 6B), and we can now see that he was already working before the mid sixth century and still at work in the time of the red-figure Pioneers. Also, new fragments of a cup foot provide further evidence that the potter Amasis (whether he was one and the same as the Amasis Painter, is still debated) was the father of the potter Kleophrades.[35] An important conference in Los Angeles shared the same title as the exhibition, and subjects in and around the painter were discussed.[36] Minor painters have also been the subject of individual articles, and a closer look given at the painters of Panathenaic amphorae.[37]

Attic Red-figure and White-ground, and Others

Work on Attic red-figure has continued unabated, particularly on the painters of the Late Archaic period. The beginnings of the new technique are still debated, the invention being ascribed to the Andokides Painter, Psiax and the Nikosthenes Painter by turns. Joan Mertens usefully emphasizes the continuity between the two techniques and sees red-figure as a revitalization of the essential ingredients which had been inherited from Geometric, with red-figure reordering line (from incision to glaze) and mass (from silhouette to reserved areas).[38] It is however the Pioneers of the late sixth century that have drawn the focus, in particular Euphronios whose works have increased in number over the past twenty years (Figs. 20 & 23). The signed Sarpedon krater in New York with Sleep and Death raising the body of the hero from the battlefield under the direction of Hermes has now become a permanent addition to the ranks of the acknowledged masterpieces of Greek vase-painting.[39] Less well known and less well preserved is the signed Kyknos krater (Fig. 20) with Athena assisting

Herakles in his struggle against the giant Kyknos, Ares' son and Thessalian bandit.[40] Euphronios' influence on later painters, whether as a painter himself or in his role as potter later in his career, has been stressed.[41] Euthymides (now known as a potter as well) and Phintias have had less of the limelight, but Phintias has been claimed as the master of the Berlin Painter who in terms of academic popularity rivals Euphronios.[42] He was a favourite of Beazley's, and Donna Kurtz has chosen him as a painter through whom Beazley's method can best be explained.[43] She has also reprinted Beazley's lecture on the artist, along with other lectures that are mainly concerned with contemporary figures. It is also through her detailed study of the Gorgos cup, excavated in the Athenian Agora and attributed by Talcott, Robertson, and reluctantly Beazley, to the Berlin Painter, that she once again applies Beazley's method, but this time to show that the cup is not his.[44] He is now claimed as the teacher of the Pan Painter, a more likely master than Myson.[45] Much has been done on the style of the Kleophrades Painter (Fig. 24),[46] and the cup painters have also been probed deeply: Onesimos (Fig. 21), the Brygos Painter, Douris, Makron, the Foundry Painter.[47]

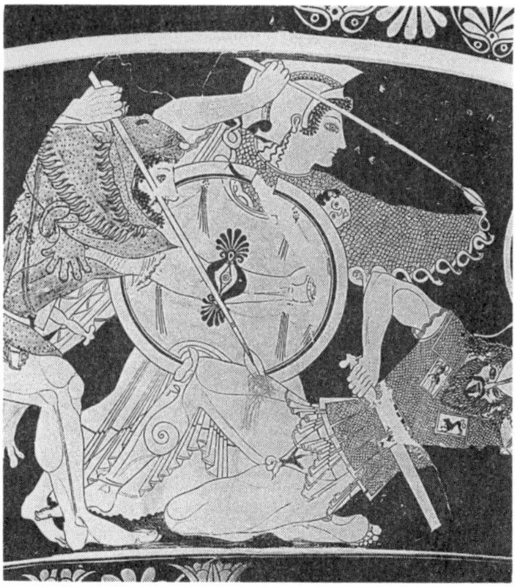

20. Herakles, Athena and Kyknos. Attic red-figure calyx-krater, signed by Euphronios. Ca. 510 B.C.

Attic white-ground continues to fascinate. The white-ground cups, mainly of the second quarter of the fifth century, are seen as special commissions, a shining example being the Apollo cup (Colour Plate 7A) that was fittingly discovered at Delphi.[48] The cups from the Sotades workshop with the delicate scenes of apple-picking, etc. have been studied afresh by a number of scholars, but more for their iconography than for their style.[49] Beazley's lecture on Attic white-ground lekythoi has been reissued,[50] and Kurtz's study of the painters and their patterns provides a basic and well-illustrated source-book of the whole range.[51]

Post-archaic red-figure still needs more attention. Boardman's recent handbook gives a useful survey of the stages of early classic, classic, late 5th century, and 4th century.[52] The early classic stage is still studied mainly from the point of view of its relation to the emerging panel paintings, and definite connections can be seen.[53] The classic stage has had the benefit of two excellent 'Kerameus' volumes from the hand of Adrienne Lezzi-Hafter, one on the Shuvalov Painter,[54] the other on The Eretria Painter and his associates.[55] The late fifth century brings us to the Meidias Painter whose work Lucilla Burn has characterized in an engaging manner, with emphasis on his subject matter (paradise gardens and such) rather than his style.[56] He and his contemporaries, both potters and painters, had an influence on the South Italian potteries, and this can be seen to very good effect on a newly discovered krater by the Meleager Painter (Fig. 22)

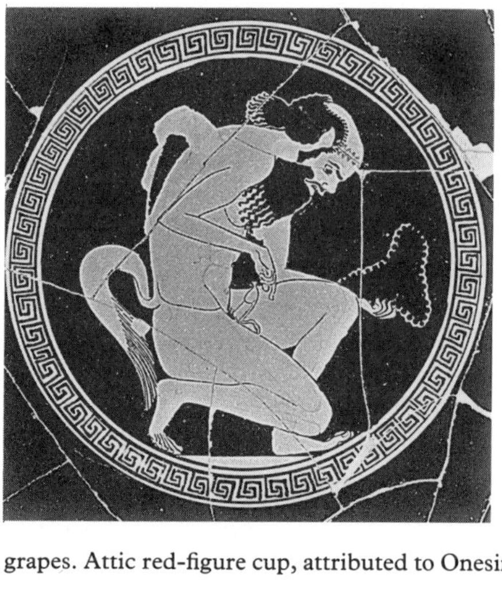

21. Satyr nibbling grapes. Attic red-figure cup, attributed to Onesimos. Ca. 500 B.C.

that bears all the hallmarks of the more ornate products of that region. It would be satisfying, though not strictly necessary, to discover the name of the Meidias Painter. An attempt to link his early work with that of Aison on the basis of a chous found in the Athenian Kerameikos has not won approval.[57] The fourth-century products of the Athenian potteries, including the 'Kerch' vases, are only now

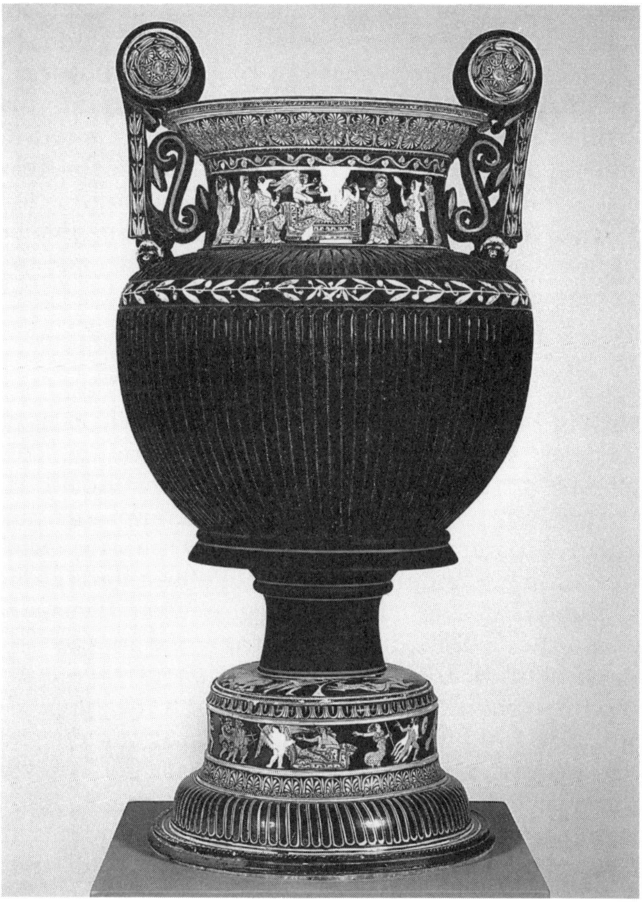

22. Adonis. Attic red-figure volute-krater and stand, attributed to the Meleager Painter. Late fifth century B.C.

receiving serious attention, after an interval of more than 50 years. Study of them shows both their relation to and their distance from the quality of the more monumental paintings that the finds from Vergina in particular have recently brought to light (Colour Plate 7B).[58]

Trendall's work of attribution on South Italian and Sicilian vases has been both broad and deep. His recent handbook is a digest of many years' patient compilation and sensitive study.[59] The picture he has built up of development in the second half of the fifth century at sites such as Metaponto and Pisticci, the growth of the Apulian school, the movement of the Sicilian painters to Campania, etc. is based on close study of stylistic details and is a vindication of the method adopted. The history that can be recreated of the Greeks in the south of Italy depends to a large extent on the information won from the painted pottery. It is doubtful whether the red-figure products of other centres (Corinth, Laconia, Chalcidice) offer much for the student of Greek art;[60] those of the Etruscans belong to the history of Etruscan art, but inevitably reflect the influence, both baleful and fascinating, that Greek vases and their craftsmen had on one of their best customers.[61]

Names, Signatures and Attribution

All who work in Beazley's shadow, whether on Attic vase-painting or on other centres, must necessarily struggle with the conventional names that have to be invented to characterize individuals. These sometimes cause scorn and derision, often incomprehension, but the need for them is paramount. More taxing are those terms used to suggest association but not identity: 'school', 'brother', 'group', 'workshop', etc. Robertson has tried to suggest what Beazley meant by such terms and their subtle differences from one another,[62] but has to admit that without Beazley's own definition of them, it is almost impossible with certain terms to tease out the meaning. How much more helpful it would have been, had the Greek potters and painters added their own names more often! We still do not know why some did and some did not – pride, personal preference, fashion – nor indeed are we quite sure of the meaning of the words they used, 'egrapsen' looks all right – 'wrote', 'drew', 'painted'; but what of 'epoiesen'? Does this signify the 'maker' of an actual piece or the more general 'proprietor' who may not have soiled his hands? New potter and painter names of Attic black- and red-figure vases are listed in the second edition of *Beazley Addenda*,[63] Beazley's 1940s lecture on 'Potter and Painter' has been reissued,[64] and there has been more recent argument on the meaning of the word 'epoiesen', with perhaps the honours going to those understanding the word as signifying the actual maker.[65] A more radical solution to the words has been proposed by Vickers who relates them to his theory that Greek clay vases were copies of metal originals (see p. 59) and would have 'egrapsen' signify the 'designer' of the composition for the metal original and 'epoiesen' the 'executant' of that original.[66] On this theory the names tell us nothing of the vase-painters, but nor does the theory deny the validity of the attributions made. In any case, the presence or absence of a name is of little direct importance, and certainly tells us nothing about quality. Let us recall that the Late Corinthian painter Khares and the Attic black-figure painter and potter Oikopheles are unspeakably poor painters; as has been asked of Khares, 'Is he not a dangerous rival to Oikopheles for the distinction of being the worst Greek vase painter who has left his name upon his work?', and one might add 'and the worst even of those who have not'.[67]

The disenchantment felt by some with the connoisseurship approach can be seen as both general and particular. Some would claim that the method is false, and that two artists can produce work that is indistinguishable from one another; that an artist can produce work varied enough not to be susceptible to such analysis; that there are no parameters to define a man's work. Others see that it is 'hard to go from formal analysis to the use of vases as documents of their time and place' and that all too often such formal study is treated as an end in itself and that there is a need to open out the study, to look at vases from the point of view of shape, subject, findspot, purpose, the place of pottery in the economic life of the Greeks.[68] Yet others see the rule of vested interests and the drawback of diminishing returns. In fact, for many the quarrel is not with Beazley, but with his epigoni.

NOTES

1. The Oxford meeting led to the publication of a small volume, *Beazley and Oxford*, in which, amongst some nostalgic pieces, Martin Robertson in 'Beazley and Attic Vase Painting' (pp. 19–30) turned his attention to present problems. The Brygos Tomb vases (Colour Plate 4A) were reassembled in the British Museum in time for the London meeting, thanks to the cooperation of Dr D. von Bothmer of the Metropolitan Museum of Art, New York, and Dr M. Maass of the Badisches Landesmuseum, Karlsruhe.

2. M. Robertson, 'Beazley and After', *MJbK* 3rd Series 27 (1976), 29–46 (quotation from 29); *Vasenforschungen nach Beazley, Tübingen 24–25.11.1978, Schriften des deutschen Archäologen-Verbandes* 4 (Mainz, 1978); H. Hoffmann, 'In the Wake of Beazley', *Hephaistos* 1 (1979), 61–70.

3. The Beazley Archive houses thousands of photographs which are constantly being added to, and 2000 drawings executed by Beazley himself. For information, see *Vasenforschung* (n. 2, above), 24–27 (D. C. Kurtz); *AK* 19 (1976), 120 and *JHS* 97 (1977), v. In *The Berlin Painter* (see n. 5, below), Kurtz publishes Beazley's drawings of the painter's work.

4. Computerized references, see *AK* 26 (1983), 106 and *JHS* 103 (1983), 160; and R. Glynn, 'The Beazley Archive computer project', *Rouen Colloque*, pp. 67–79. *Beazley Addenda* contains additions to Beazley, *Attic Black-Figure Vase-Painters* (Oxford, 1956), *Attic Red-Figure Vase-Painters*, 2nd edition (Oxford, 1963) and *Paralipomena*, ed. M. Robertson (Oxford, 1971).

5. D. C. Kurtz, *The Berlin Painter* (Oxford, 1983); 'Beazley and the Connoisseurship of Greek Vases', *Greek Vases* II (1985), 237–50. In *The Berlin Painter*, p. 12, Kurtz points out that Beazley never once mentioned Morelli, the 'father' of the method Beazley adopted. See also M. Robertson in the introduction to *Beazley Addenda*. For a brief account of connoisseurship, see D. von Bothmer, 'Greek Vase-painting: two hundred years of connoisseurship', *Amasis Painter, Papers*, pp. 184–204.

6. 'The place of vase-painting in Greek art', *BSA* 46 (1951), 151–9.

7. *MJbK* 3rd series 27 (1976), 35. Some of Beazley's contributions to the pre-war series of German monographs under the general title of 'Bilder Griechische Vasen' which he and Paul

Jacobsthal edited, have recently been reissued with Beazley's original English texts: *The Kleophrades Painter* (Mainz, 1974), *The Pan Painter* (Mainz, 1974).

8. Quotations from *Beazley and Oxford*, p. 27, and *MJbK* 3rd series 27 (1976), 36.

9. See M. Robertson, 'The State of Attic Vase-Painting in the Mid Sixth Century', *Amasis Painter, Papers*, pp. 13–28.

10. The basic study of Geometric by painters and regions is N. Coldstream, *Greek Geometric Pottery* (London, 1968).

11. J. L. Benson, *Earlier Corinthian Workshops, A Survey of Corinthian Geometric and Protocorinthian Stylistic Groups* (Allard Pierson Series, Scripta Minora 1, Amsterdam, 1989). See also J. L. Benson's editing of A. N. Stillwell's volume on the Potters' Quarter, *The Potters' Quarter: the Pottery, Corinth* XV, part iii (Princeton, 1984). D. A. Amyx, *Corinthian Vase-Painting of the Archaic Period*, 3 vols. (California Studies in the History of Art XXV, University of California Press, 1988).

12. S. P. Morris, *The Black and White Style, Athens and Aegina in the Orientalizing Period* (Yale University Press, 1984). For a more general investigation of 7th century Attica and a characterization of the difference between Geometric and Protoattic artistic expression, see R. Osborne, 'A crisis in archaeological history? The seventh century B.C. in Attica', *BSA* 84 (1989), 297–322. For the beginning of polychrome painting in the seventh century, see G. P. Schaus, 'The beginning of Greek polychrome painting', *JHS* 108 (1988), 107–17, pls. 3–4.

13. The Northampton Group: E. Langlotz, *Studien zur nordostgriechischen Kunst* (Mainz, 1975); E. Walter-Karydi, *CVA* Munich 6 (28), 42–6; J. Boardman, *CVA* Castle Ashby (15), 1–2; E. Simon and M. and M. Hirmer, *Die griechischen Vasen* (Munich, 1981), pp. 61–2, pls. XVI–XVII.

14. R. M. Cook, *Clazomenian Sarcophagi* (Kerameus 3, Mainz, 1981) and 'A Clazomenian sarcophagus in Geneva', *AK* 30 (1987), 156–7, pl. 22. And see E. Kirchner, 'Zum Bildprogramm Klazomenischer Sarkophage', *JDAI* 102 (1987), 119–61.

15. J. M. Hemelrijk, *Caeretan Hydriai* (Kerameus 5, Mainz, 1984). And see *Greek Vases from the Hirschmann Collection*, ed. H. Bloesch (Zurich, 1982), nos. 10–12; H. P. Isler, 'Drei neue Gefässe aus der Werkstatt der Caeretaner Hydrien', *JDAI* 98 (1983), 15–56. For the hero of Colour Plate 4B as Herakles, see J. Boardman, 'Very like a whale – classical sea monsters', *Monsters and Demons in the Ancient and Medieval Worlds. Papers presented in honor of Edith Porada*, edd. A. E. Farkas, P. O. Harper and E. B. Harrison (Mainz, 1987), pp. 73–84, pls. 21–6.

16. C. M. Stibbe, *Lakonische Vasenmaler des sechsten Jahrhunderts v. Chr.* (Amsterdam–London, 1972).

17. N. Spivey, *The Micali Painter and his Followers* (Oxford, 1987) (quotations from p. 49). There was also an exhibition at the Villa Giulia in Rome (and a catalogue) to celebrate the painter: *Un artista etrusco e il suo mondo: Il pittore di Micali* (Rome, 1988). See now R. M. Cook, 'East Greek influences on Etruscan vase-painting', *La Parola del Passato* 246 (1989), 161–73.

18. J. Boardman, *Athenian Black Figure Vases, a handbook* (London, 1974). Note that the word 'Athenian' is used, not 'Attic'.

19. J. Boardman, *Athenian Red Figure Vases, the Archaic Period, a handbook* (London, 1975).

20. J. Boardman, *Athenian Red Figure Vases, the Classical Period, a handbook* (London, 1989). R. Folsom's two volumes, *Attic black-figured pottery* (Park Ridge, 1975) and *Attic red-figured pottery* (Park Ridge, 1976) are much less helpful and accurate than Boardman's.

21. *The Development of Attic Black-figure*, 2nd ed., revised and edited by D. von Bothmer and M. B. Moore (Berkeley, 1986).

22. 'Attic Black-figure; a sketch', now in *Beazley Lectures*, pp. 1–25, 103–6, pls. 1–16.

23. *Beazley Addenda*, 2nd ed., pp. 1–148. M. B. Moore and M. Z. P. Philippides, *Attic Black-Figured Pottery* (*The Athenian Agora*, vol. 23, Princeton, 1986) looks at shapes and painters. J. R. Mertens, 'Some thoughts on Attic vase-painting of the 6th cent. B.C.', *Copenhagen Symposium*, pp. 414–34, has a close look at sixth century Attic vase-painting.

24. G. Bakir, *Sophilos: Ein Beitrag zu seinem Stil* (Keramikforschungen 4, Mainz, 1981).

25. Dyfri Williams, 'Sophilos in the British Museum', *Greek Vases* I (1983), 9–34.

26. A. F. Stewart, 'Stesichoros and the François Vase', Moon *AGAI*, pp. 53–74. Against the

connection with Stesichoros, see J. R. March, *The Creative Poet* (*BICS* Supplementary Volume 49, 1987), 4, n. 12.

27. M. Cristofani, *Materiali per servire alla storia del Vaso François, Bollettino d'Arte* Serie Speciale 1 (Rome, 1980).

28. M. Tiverios, *Ὁ Λυδὸς καὶ τὸ ἔργο του* (Athens, 1976). See also M. B. Moore, 'Lydos and the Gigantomachy', *AJA* 83 (1979), 79–99, pls. 11–15.

29. On the dating and provenance of Tyrrhenian amphorae, see T. H. Carpenter, 'On the dating of the Tyrrhenian Group', *OJA* 2 (1983), 279–293, and 'The Tyrrhenian Group: problems of provenance', 3 (1984), 45–56. For a detailed investigation of the relation between Lydos and the painters of Tyrrhenian amphorae, see H. A. Shapiro, 'Two black-figure neck-amphorae in the J. Paul Getty Museum: problems of workshop and iconography', *Greek Vases* IV (1989), 11–32.

30. H. A. G. Brijder, *Siana Cups I and Komast Cups* (Amsterdam, 1983).

31. Exekias: M. Robertson, 'A new plaque-fragment by Exekias', *ArchEph* 1978, 91–4, pl. 33; J. Boardman, 'Exekias', *AJA* 82 (1978), 11–25; M. B. Moore, 'Exekias and Telamonian Ajax', *AJA* 84 (1980), 417–34; H. A. Shapiro, 'Exekias, Ajax and Salamis: a further note', *AJA* 85 (1981), 173–5; M. B. Moore, 'The death of Pedasos', *AJA* 86 (1982), 578–81, pl. 76; 'Exekias and the harnessing of a chariot team', *AK* 29 (1986), 107–114, pl. 19; 'The Amasis Painter and Exekias: approaches to narrative', *Amasis Painter, Papers*, pp. 153–167.

32. H. Mommsen, *Der Affekter* (Kerameus 1, Mainz, 1975).

33. E. Böhr, *Der Schaukelmaler* (Kerameus 4, Mainz, 1982). See now E. Böhr 'Weitere Werke des Schaukelmalers', *Praestant Interna*, 213–20, pls. 44–6 and D. von Bothmer's review, *AJA* 89 (1985), 362.

34. *Amasis Painter, Catalogue.*

35. D. von Bothmer, '*Ἄμασις, Ἀμάσιδος*', *GettyMJ* 9 (1981), 1–4.

36. *Amasis Painter, Papers.*

37. E.g. D. von Bothmer, 'Elbows Out', *RA* 1969, 3–15; E. Moignard, 'The Acheloos Painter and his relations', *BSA* 77 (1982), 201–11, pls. 7–14; W. G. Moon, 'The Priam Painter: some iconographic and stylistic considerations', Moon *AGAI*, pp. 97–118; *Greek Vase-Painting in Midwestern Collections*, ed. W. G. Moon (Chicago, 1979), pp. 50–56 (The Painter of Berlin 1686). See now a new Kerameus volume, J. Burow, *Der Antimenesmaler* (Kerameus 7, Mainz, 1990). When will the major figures be introduced?

For work on the Panathenaics, see J. Frel, *Panathenaic Prize Amphoras* (Athens, 1973); J. R. Brandt, 'Archaeologica Panathenaica I: Panathenaic prize amphorae from the sixth century B.C.', *Acta ad archaeologiam et artium historiam pertinentia, Institutum Romanum Norvegiae et Oslo, Universitëtsforl* 8 (1978), 1–23; N. Eschbach, *Statuen auf Panathenäischen Preisamphoren des 4. Jhs v. Chr.* (Mainz, 1985). See also n. 46 below.

38. On Psiax, see J. L. Mertens, 'Some new vases by Psiax', *AK* 22 (1979), 22–37, pls. 9–14, and on the continuity between black- and red-figure, *Copenhagen Symposium*, pp. 414–34. And see now B. Cohen, 'Oddities of very early red-figure and a new fragment at the Getty', *Greek Vases* IV (1989), 73–82.

39. D. von Bothmer, 'Der Euphronioskrater in New York', *AA* 1976, 485–512, and 'The Death of Sarpedon', *The Greek Vase*, ed. S. L. Hyatt (Hudson Valley, 1981), pp. 63–80, 156–58, figs. 65–87. See also 'Euphronios and Memnon? Observations on a red-figured fragment', *MMJ* 22 (1987), 5–11.

40. M. Ohly-Dumm, 'Euphroniosschale und Smikrosscherbe', *MJbK* 25 (1974), 7–26; M. Robertson, 'Euphronios at the Getty', *GettyMJ* 9 (1981), 23–34, esp. 29–34, and H. A. Shapiro, 'Herakles and Kyknos', *AJA* 88 (1984), 523–9, pls. 68–9.

41. M. Ohly-Dumm, 'Medeas Widderzauber auf einer Schale aus der Werkstatt des Euphronios', *GettyMJ* 9 (1981), 5–21; B. A. Sparkes, 'Aspects of Onesimos', *Greek Art: Archaic into Classical, a symposium held at the University of Cincinnati April 2–3, 1982*, ed. C. G. Boulter (Leiden, 1985), pp. 18–39, pls. 19–36. See now *L'arte di Eufronio* (Florence, 1990)

42. M. Ohly-Dumm, 'Sosias und Euthymides', *Amsterdam Symposium*, 165–72; G. F. Pinney, 'The nonage of the Berlin Painter, *AJA* 85 (1981), 145–58, pls. 29–36; C. Weiss, 'Phintias in Malibu und Karlsruhe', *Greek Vases* IV (1989), 83–94.

43. D. C. Kurtz, *The Berlin Painter* (Oxford, 1983). See also M. Robertson, 'A neck-

amphora by the Berlin Painter', *MJbK* 31 (1980), 7–12 and 'The Berlin Painter at the Getty and some others', *Greek Vases* I (1983), 55–72.

44. J. D. Beazley, 'The Berlin Painter', now in *Beazley Lectures*, pp. 66–77, 117–8, pls. 38–47. D. C. Kurtz, 'Gorgos' cup: an essay in connoisseurship, *JHS* 103 (1983), 68–86, pls. 3–9.

45. C. Sourvinou-Inwood, 'Who was the teacher of the Pan Painter?', *JHS* 95 (1975) 107–121, pls. 9–11. See also M. Robertson, 'Two pelikai by the Pan Painter', *Greek Vases III* (1986), 71–90.

46. A. Greifenhagen, *Neue Fragmente des Kleophradesmalers* (SBer. Heidelberg, 1972, 4); J. Boardman, 'The Kleophrades Painter's cup in London', *GettyMJ* 1 (1974), 7–14 and 'The Kleophrades Painter at Troy', *AK* 19 (1976), 3–18, pls. 1–3; M. Robertson, 'An unrecognized cup by the Kleophrades Painter?', *ΣΤΗΛΗ, Τόμος εἰς μνήμην Νικολάου Κοντολέοντος* (Athens, 1980), pp. 125–9, pls. 43–4 and 'Fragments of a dinos and a cup fragment by the Kleophrades Painter', *Greek Vases* 1 (1983), 51–4; S. B. Matheson, 'Panathenaic amphorae by the Kleophrades Painter', *Greek Vases* IV (1989), 95–112. The signature 'Epiktetos' is now shown to be false, see J. Boardman and U. Gehrig, 'Epiktetos II R.I.P.', *AA* 1981, 329–32.

47. Onesimos: D. Williams, 'The Ilioupersis cup in Berlin and the Vatican', *JBerlMuseum* 18 (1976), 9–23; 'Ajax, Odysseus and the arms of Achilles', *AK* 23 (1980), 137–45, pls. 33–6: and see n. 41 above. Douris: D. Buitron, *Douris* (University Microfilms, Ann Arbor, Michigan, 1976). The Brygos Painter: M. Wegner, *Brygosmaler* (Berlin, 1973); A. Cambitoglou, *The Brygos Painter* (Sydney University Press, 1968); D. Williams, 'An oinochoe in the British Museum and the Brygos Painter's work on a white ground), *JBerlMuseum* 22 (1982), 17–40. Makron: D. von Bothmer, 'Notes on Makron', *Eye of Greece*, pp. 29–52, pls. 7–13, and Beazley's previously unpublished lecture, now in *Beazley Lectures*, pp. 84–97, 118–20, pls. 65–80. The Foundry Painter: J. D. Beazley, 'A Greek Realist', now in *Beazley Lectures*, pp. 78–83, 118, pls. 48–64.

48. J. R. Mertens, *Attic White-Ground: its development on shapes other than lekythoi* (New York, 1977) and 'Attic white-ground cups: a special class of vases', *MMJ* 9 (1974), 91–108; I. Wehgartner, *Attisch Weissgrundige Keramik* (Mainz, 1983). For the Delphi Apollo cup, see H. Metzger, '*'Απόλλων σπένδων*', *BCH* Supplement 4 (1977), 421–8.

49. L. Burn, 'Honey pots: three white-ground cups by the Sotades Painter', *AK* 28 (1985), 93–105, pls. 23–27 and colour pl. A; A. Griffiths, '"What leaf-fringed legend . . . ?" A cup by the Sotades Painter in London', *JHS* 106 (1986), 58–70, pls. 1–3; A. Collinge, 'Aristaios, or his father-in-law', *AK* 31 (1988), 9–20, pl. 3.

50. J. D. Beazley, 'Attic White Lekythoi', now in *Beazley Lectures*, pp. 26–38, 107–9, pls. 17–24.

51. D. C. Kurtz, *Athenian White Lekythoi, Patterns and Painters* (Oxford, 1975). See also I. Wehgartner, *Ein Grabbild des Achilleusmalers* (Berlin, 1985) for an early and innovatory lekythos by the Achilles Painter. See now D. C. Kurtz, 'Two Athenian white-ground lekythoi', *Greek Vases* IV (1989), 113–30.

52. J. Boardman, *Athenian Red Figure Vases, the Classical Period, a handbook* (London, 1989).

53. J. P. Barron, 'New light on old walls: the murals of the Theseion', *JHS* 92 (1972), 20–45, pls. 1–7; S. Woodford, 'More light on old walls: the Theseus of the Centauromachy in the Theseion', *JHS* 94 (1974), 158–65, pls. 14–15; M. D. Stansbury-O'Donnell, 'Polygnotos' Iliupersis: a new reconstruction', *AJA* 93 (1989), 203–15. On the Niobid Painter, see M. Prange, *Der Niobidenmaler und seine Werkstatt* (Frankfurt, 1989).

54. A. Lezzi-Hafter, *Der Schuwalowmaler. Ein Kannenwerkstatt der Parthenonzeit* (Kerameus 2, Mainz, 1982).

55. A. Lezzi-Hafter, *Der Eretria-maler, Werke und Weggefährten* (Kerameus 6, Mainz, 1988). See also J. H. Oakley, *The Phiale Painter* (Kerameus 8, Mainz, 1990).

56. L. Burn, *The Meidias Painter* (Oxford, 1987). See also M. True, 'A new Meidian kylix', *Greek Vases* II (1985), 79–88. New volute-krater, *GettyMJ* 16 (1988), 143, no. 7. For good comments on late fifth-century work, see B. B. Shefton, 'The krater from Baksy', *Eye of Greece*, pp. 149–81. Dr Burn, who made the attribution of Fig 22 to the Meleager Painter, is to publish a study of it shortly. I am grateful to her for her cooperation.

57. U. Knigge, 'Aison, der Meidiasmaler? Zu einer rotfigurigen Oinochoe aus dem Kerameikos', *AM* 90 (1975), 123–43, pls. 43–51.

58. Dr Antoine Lebel has recently worked fruitfully on the fourth-century painters for an Oxford DPhil. For fourth-century tomb-painting, see P. Petsas, '*Ο Τάφος τῶν Λευκαδίων* (Athens, 1966) and M. Andronikos, *Vergina* (Athens, 1984).

59. A. D. Trendall, *Red Figure Vases of South Italy and Sicily, a handbook* (Thames and Hudson, 1989). The work of M. Schmidt and A. Cambitoglou is also of prime importance. See also the exhibition catalogue *The Art of South Italy: Vases from Magna Graecia*, ed. M. E. Mayo (Virginia, 1982).

60. Laconia: I. McPhee, 'Laconian red-figure from the British excavations in Sparta', *BSA* 81 (1986), 153–64, pls. 3–7, and 153, n. 6 for other local red-figure. Corinth: S. Herbert, *Corinth, American School Excavations* VII part iv *The red-figure pottery* (Princeton, 1977) and I. McPhee, 'Local red-figure from Corinth 1973–1980', *Hesperia* 52 (1983), 137–53, pls. 33–41. Chalcidice: I. McPhee, 'Some red-figure vase-painters of the Chalcidice', *BSA* 76 (1981), 297–308, pls. 49–53.

61. For a general picture book of Etruscan pottery, see M. Martelli, *La ceramica degli Etruschi, la pittura vascolare* (Novara, 1987).

62. *Beazley Addenda*, xi–xviii (1st edition) and xii–xx (2nd edition). Beazley's talk of 'follower', 'school', 'influence' on the basis of a Renaissance model has been decried as converting 'what had been the subject of antiquarian interest into high status art history' (M. Beard, *TLS* 12.9.86, 1013).

63. *Beazley Addenda* (2nd edition), pp. 400–406.

64. J. D. Beazley, 'Potter and Painter in Ancient Athens', now in *Beazley Lectures*, pp. 39–59, 109–16, pls. 25–32.

65. R. M. Cook, '"Epoiesen" on Greek vases', *JHS* 91 (1971), 137–8; M. Robertson, '"Epoiesen" on Greek vases: other considerations', *JHS* 92 (1972), 189–83; M. M. Eisman, 'A further note on *ΕΠΟΙΕΣΕΝ* signatures', *JHS* 94 (1974), 172. And see H. Immerwahr, *Attic Script* (Oxford, 1990).

66. M. J. Vickers, 'Artful crafts: the influence of metalwork on Athenian painted pottery', *JHS* 105 (1985), 108–28, pls. 4–6.

67. H. G. G. Payne, *Necrocorinthia* (Oxford, 1931), 322.

68. For a severe critique, see P. Bruneau, 'Situation méthodologique de l'histoire de l'art antique', *L'antiquité classique* 44 (1975), 425–87. Quotation from G. F. Pinney, *AJA* 88 (1984), 420.

V. SHOPS AND SHAPES

Shops

Admiration for the quality and appearance of Greek pottery, and interest in the subject matter of the figured scenes, have until recently tended to draw attention away from other aspects of the study. In reaction to what is seen as an overemphasis on attribution, both of painters and of potters, one approach which has been adopted is to consider the organization of the shops which produced the pottery, to see the pottery in its sociological context.[1] Talk of 'pupils', 'masters', 'influence' etc. presupposes that we know the arrangements under which the potters and painters worked, but hard facts are few.

There is evidence from excavated kilns, but the workshops which lay nearby and their spatial organization are less well known.[2] The Potters' Quarter at Corinth gives a better idea than other sites of this aspect, but there are no kilns there, and we do not know how typical the Potters' Quarter was – there were other areas of production at Corinth.[3] A workshop find such as that of the Jena Painter in Athens has given only a little help.[4] Literary references are sparse, more helpful are the representations on vases, but these are few and limited in the information they provide. How literal we must understand them to be in the number and sex of the workers, the types of vases being produced, etc. is difficult to decide.[5] Certainly, the conventions of vase-painting preclude background detail.

The results of the attribution of vases to individual potters and painters have given some indication of what may be the larger sizes of workshop: a score of painters working in the Penthesilea Painter's workshop in scarcely more than a generation, a dozen or more painters having 'made by Nikosthenes' on their pots, two hundred working in Athens at any one time (with presumably some of those part-time and/or temporary). Influence from older man to younger, and rivalry between potters and painters (between Exekias and Amasis, if not between Euphronios and Euthymides), suggests proximity, but this may be either within or between workshops. Many shops must have been one-man or family concerns, and Athens was certainly not a typical centre of pottery production.[6] Signatures tell us more of the idiosyncrasies of the practitioners of the craft and their search perhaps for prestige. Where a father is mentioned (Kleophrades, son of Amasis, or Tleson and Ergokles, sons of Nearkhos), this can be seen 'not merely as an act of filial piety but also a useful advertisement to his customers, both domestic and foreign'.[7]

The price of vases, usually to be found as 'trademarks' under the feet of Athenian pieces that went westwards, shows us how cheap they were at some stage in the transactions – three drachmas for a red-figure hydria is the most expensive, a cup or a lekythos may have cost about one drachma.[8] Their value in non-money terms may have been different – mends and the difference in dates of vases in a single tomb, e.g. the Brygos Tomb (Colour Plate 4A), may show that someone cared for them over a period of time.[9] The economic value tends to be set low. Most vases would have been made for the local market, and those that did travel may not have been leading items. Those who did see pottery as making a mark on the economy of a state are uniformly castigated nowadays. Agricultural produce, metals, timber and such were the main items, and mixed with these, as the excavated shipwrecks show more and more, was pottery, some for their contents (such as transport amphorae), others for themselves.[10] A secondhand market for pottery now seems to be thought unlikely,[11] and the extent to which pottery either in shapes or subject matter was tailored for a 'foreign' market, is hard to gauge – Nikosthenes' special lines for Etruria, stemmed plates to Spina, Persian subjects found in Persia, Arimasps and griffins in the far north-east – how should such specific items be understood?[12] The whole question of who paid the potter and called the tune is a difficult one to answer.

Emphasis has recently been laid on the humble nature of the craft of pottery, its simple mechanics, the cheapness of the materials, the narrow profits, its production in vast numbers, the slave names of its practitioners, whether potter or painter,[13] a lack of regard that the absence of references from literature would suggest. No rich patrons are thought likely to have commissioned special orders from such shops – it was not a high-status industry, though it had surely been so in Geometric times. The late sixth-century 'Pioneer' group in Athens in which Euphronios calls a symposiast 'Smikros' (Fig. 23), Smikros names an athlete 'Euphronios' and himself a symposiast, and Phintias calls a music student 'Euthymides', are judged by some as scenes of wish fulfilment. The picture that has in the past been recreated of potters hobnobbing with the aristocracy is beginning to be questioned. Also in doubt is the identity of those who set up the 'kerameus' dedications on the Athenian Akropolis. Where 'kerameus' is found in inscriptions, can it not be interpreted, it is asked, as a reference to an inhabitant of the deme 'Kerameis', of which we know the aristocrat Leagros himself to have been a member.[14] There is much work yet to be done in this area.

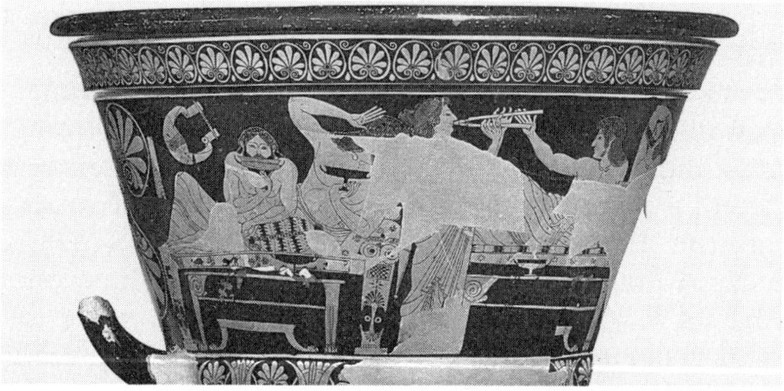

23. Smikros at a symposium. Attic red-figure calyx-krater, attributed to Euphronios. Ca. 500 B.C.

Shapes

The shapes of Greek pottery have not been studied with the same degree of intensity as the scenes they carry. The study of the aesthetics of their forms seems to be more attractive to German scholars than to others.[15] However, the details of the shapes, their development, the interrelationships between different centres of production, the individual hands of the potters, the functions of the vases, etc. have all been investigated.[16]

What has proved one of the most argued aspects in the scholarly literature recently is the relationship of pottery shapes and decoration to those in other materials, especially metal. That potters borrowed ideas for shapes from other materials is not in doubt: wood lies behind such a shape as the pyxis (indeed, the similarity of the carpenter's lathe technique has recently been stressed),[17] basketwork for the kalathos, horn for the rhyton, stone for the alabastron, leather for the aryballos. However, the liveliest, not to say the most acrimonious, debate has centred on the connection between Attic archaic and classical pottery and metal work, whether gold, silver, or bronze. Here again the dependence is in some instances clear – the lebes/dinos is metal-inspired, the beak-spout oinochoe is influenced by metal prototypes, the phiale is another example of a metal shape copied in clay.[18] Also, the details such as studs, rivets, rotelles and various shapes of handles and feet, proclaim the connection. But some would now take the relationship much further and with far-reaching consequences.[19]

The main points seem to be:

Although little silver is preserved in Greece itself in the form of vases, literature and epigraphy indicate that there was a great deal of it in the fifth century, particularly as a consequence of the Persian Wars and of the silver strike made at the beginning of the century at Laurium. That the major finds of silver and silver-gilt pieces have been made in the North (Macedonia, e.g. at Vergina and Derveni; Bulgaria, e.g. at Duvanlij and Rogozen (Colour Plate 8C); and South Russia (Colour Plate 8B)[20]) stems from the fact that the Thracians and Skythians buried the precious objects with their dead, whereas in Greece pottery surrogates were buried instead, the precious metals being kept for the use and abuse of the living.[21] Thus we are urged to think of the Athenians as living in accordance with a silver-standard, and the pottery as cheap facsimiles.

It is suggested that in shapes the correspondence between metal and pottery is more widespread than had been realized, with the influence always from the more precious material to the cheaper. Not only is this to be seen in the matter of shapes (Colour Plate 8A) but also in such treatment as ribbing which enhances the reflected glitter of metal[22] and even in incised patterns and scenes (Colour plate 8B), and in stamping. Designs were, it is claimed, passed down from metal workers to potters, to be slavishly copied in clay.

The thesis goes further than this and applies the relationship to the colours of pottery decoration as well. The black is seen as tarnished silver (the way, it is claimed, the Greeks preferred it), the red is first bronze, then gold, so that early black-figure counterfeits silver on bronze, later black-figure silver on gold and red-figure gold on silver. To add to this, the theory has the white on white-ground vases as a substitute for ivory, and purple for copper inlay for strengthening.[23]

Various consequences flow from this, not least that much scholarly effort has been expended on cheap imitations in shape and decoration for which exaggerated claims have been made. The names we have (not to mention the personalities to whom names have been given) are on this new thesis the names of the designers ('egrapsen') and the executants of the designs ('epoiesen'), and thus the pottery versions are copies, and the names and styles do not belong to the potters and vase-painters. The subject matter of the contemporary scenes which refer chiefly to the life of the Athenian aristocracy (one thinks of symposia, in particular, e.g. Fig. 23), falls into place as originally created for the more expensive material that the aristocrats would have been using at their tables.[24]

The theory is also seen to account for the demise of the decoration on pottery in the late fourth century when the Eastern preference for relief decoration in metalwork killed the market in incised silverware. There are also other, more detailed elements in the theory that are felt to account for what have been puzzling aspects of painted pottery.

Such a daring theory has not gone unchallenged; some of the objections to it are:[25]

There are no examples of bronze or gold vases with silver figures, no silver vases with gilt figures until the late fifth century and no copper strengthening on silver vases. The passage on which the claim that the Greeks preferred to have their silver black is based, is thought to render quite the opposite meaning, and the context is shown to present the idea of 'silver is black' as a paradox. Much play has been made of Thetis and Aphrodite (each 'arguropeza') with black feet. The dependence of potters on metal has been felt to have been exaggerated, and it is suggested that some of the metal connections that have been posited point rather in the direction of wood.

Questions are asked, such as: why was never more than one copy of each silver design created? It would seem a prodigal waste of talent not to produce duplicates. Why are different strengths of line (such as dilute and relief line) used on painted pottery, when they are not possible on metal? As precise copies would not give room for experiments, how is one to account for the presence of preliminary sketches ('pentimenti') on pottery? Why was real gold added to enhance the pots on later red-figure, when the red was already in imitation of gold? Indeed, how close is the red to the gold or the purple to the copper, even if we leave aside the problem of silver and black? Given the popularity of gold and silver phialai, why are there so few in clay that have survived? To whom did the silver belong? Surely not the silversmiths. Were they perhaps as much the banausoi as the potters? Are we to assume that the aristocrats never used clay?

The epoiesen–egrapsen thesis is shown not to work in every case, as we know of a Bakkhios who made Panathenaic amphorae in the fourth century and was certainly working in clay, as his tombstone speaks of him as the best 'of those who blend earth, water, and fire into one by art'. It has also been pointed out that there is no reason for 'epoiesen' in its new meaning to be set on those vases which carry no design, yet some are known on clay vases. In more general terms, many find it hard to understand the historical development that is being suggested. Pottery-making and decorating in Geometric times was an important craft and owed nothing to metalworking – where does the change occur, when did the highjacking of the pottery shops take place? Or is it 'more a case of like ideals than of direct copying'?[26]

The debate continues, and a serious scholarly division has been created that deeply affects our perception of the pottery industry in Athens, not to mention the social background against which the vases were produced.

NOTES

1. See K. Arafat and C. Morgan, 'Pots and Potters in Athens and Corinth: a review', *OJA* 8 (1989), 31–46.

2. For organization, see D. P. S. Peacock, *Pottery in the Roman World: an ethnoarchaeological approach* (London, 1982); I. Scheibler, *Griechische Töpferkunst* (Munich, 1983); R. E. Jones, *Greek and Cypriot Pottery, a review of Scientific Studies* (Athens, 1986); P. M. Rice, *Pottery Analysis, a sourcebook* (Chicago, 1987); K. Arafat and C. Morgan (n. 1, above), 314–7, 321–5 and 342, n. 2 (for new kilns found in Athens). There is also a new edition of J. V. Noble, *The Techniques of Painted Attic Pottery* (London, 1988).

3. A. N. Stillwell, *The Potters' Quarter: The Pottery, Corinth* XV, part iii, ed. J. L. Benson (Princeton, 1984).

4. Found in Hermes Steet at the end of the last century (Beazley, *ARV*², 1510–11).

5. J. D. Beazley, 'Potter and Painter in ancient Athens', *Beazley Lectures*, pp. 39–59, 109–16, pls. 25–32; J. Ziomecki, *Les représentations d'artisans sur les vases antiques* (Warsaw, 1975); I. Kehrberg, 'The potter-painter's wife', *Hephaistos* 4 (1982), 25–35, pl. 1; N. Cuomo di Caprio, 'Pottery kilns on pinakes from Corinth', *Amsterdam Symposium*, pp. 72–82; K. Arafat and C. Morgan (n. 1, above), 317–9.

6. R. M. Cook, 'Die Bedeutung der bemalten Keramik für den griechischen Handel', *JDAI* 74 (1959), 114–23; K. Arafat and C. Morgan (n. 1, above), 326–9 and 320–1 (Exekias v. Amasis); Beazley, *ARV*², pp. 877–9 (Penthesilea Workshop). For Euphronios versus Euthymides, see G. Neumann, 'Zu einigen Beischriften auf Münchener Vasen', *AA* 1977, 39–41, figs. 2a–3b and A. Linfert, 'Zwei Versuche über antiken Witz und Esprit', *Rivista di Archeologia* 1 (1977), 19–22, fig. 1–4. For a family business, see J. L. Hemelrijk, *Caeretan Hydriai* (Mainz, 1984), 66–9. On the urban emphasis of painted pottery, see R. Osborne, *Classical Landscape with Figures* (London, 1987), p. 109.

7. Quotation from D. von Bothmer, *GettyMJ* 9 (1981), 4; K. Arafat and C. Morgan (n. 1, above), 319–21; J. Mertens, *Copenhagen Symposium*, 425–30, insists on the importance of those signatures that we have.

8. A. W. Johnston, *Trademarks on Greek Vases* (Warminster, 1979). The 'price war' rages, see most recently, D. W. J. Gill, 'Silver anchors and cargoes of oil: some observations on Phoenician trade in the Western Mediterranean', *PBSR* 43 (1988), 1–12, esp. 2–4.

9. Heirlooms: *Beazley Lectures*, pp. 84–85; D. Williams, *Greek Vases* (London, 1985), pp. 45–8 (the Brygos tomb); M. Vickers and A. Bazama, 'A fifth century B.C. tomb in Cyrenaica', *Libya Antiqua* 8 (1971), 69–85 (Panathenaic).

10. Some recent articles on distribution and trade: J. Boardman, 'The Athenian pottery trade', *Expedition* 1979, 33–40; D. J. W. Gill, 'The distribution of Greek vases and long distance trade', *Copenhagen Symposium*, pp. 175–85; L. Hannestad, 'The Athenian potter and the home market', *Copenhagen Symposium*, pp. 222–30; J. Boardman, 'Trade in Greek decorated pottery', *OJA* 7 (1988), 27–33; D. W. J. Gill, 'Trade in Greek decorated pottery: some corrections', *OJA* 7 (1988), 369–70; J. Boardman, 'The trade figures', *OJA* 7 (1988), 371–3.

11. Secondhand: T. B. L. Webster, *Potter and Patron in Classical Athens* (London, 1972), ch. 20; I. Scheibler, *Griechische Töpferkunst* (Munich, 1983), part 3.

12. Nikosthenes: T. Rasmussen, 'Etruscan shapes in Attic pottery', *AK* 28 (1985), 33–9, pl. 13; Persian subjects: K. de Vries, 'Attic pottery in the Achaemenid Empire', *AJA* 81 (1977), 544–8. See also J. de la Genière, 'Les acheteurs des cratères corinthiens', *BCH* 112 (1988), 83–90.

13. For possible slave names, see Brygos, Skythes, Onesimos, Epiktetos, and see F. Canciani, 'Lydos, der Sklave?', *AK* 21 (1978), 17–22, pl. 6.

14. Kerameus (= of the deme Kerameis), M. J. Vickers, 'Les vases peints: image ou mirage', *Rouen Colloque*, pp. 29–42, esp. 39; 'Artful crafts: the influence of metalwork on Athenian painted pottery', *JHS* 105 (1985), 124–5. For the more traditional view, see *Beazley Lectures*, pp. 48–9; T. B. L. Webster, *Potter and Patron in Classical Athens* (London, 1972), pp. 4–7; I. Scheibler, 'Griechische Künstlervotive der archaischen Zeit', *MJbK* 30 (1979), 7–30; A. W. Johnston, *AJA* 89 (1985), 182; *Amasis Painter, Papers*, pp. 84–5 (Ridgway) and 135–6 (Johnston); K. Arafat and C. Morgan (n. 1, above), 312. See M. Vickers, 'Imaginary Etruscans: changing perceptions of Etruria since the fifteenth century', *Hephaistos* 7/8 (1985–6), 153–68

and 'Value and simplicity: eighteenth-century taste and the study of Greek vases', *Past and Present* 116 (1987), 98–137, for a view of how the status of painted pottery was falsely (and fraudently) raised in the 18th century.

15. H. Sichtermann, *Die griechische Vase: Gestalt, Sinn und Kunstwerk* (Berlin, 1963); W. Schiering, *Die griechische Tongefässe: Gestalt, Bestimmung und Formenwandel* (2nd ed., Berlin, 1983).

16. M. G. Kanowski, *Containers of Classical Greece: a handbook of shapes* (University of Queensland Press, 1984) is useful on the names and uses of the shapes, though the illustrations vary in quality. J. Boardman's three handbooks on Athenian black- and red-figure (IV, nn. 18–20) have useful chapters and bibliographies on shapes, as does Trendall's handbook on South Italian (IV, n. 59).

17. J. Boardman, 'Silver is white', *RA* 1987, 289–93. For a reply, see D. W. J. Gill and M. Vickers, 'Pots and kettles', *RA* 1989, 297–303, esp. 299–300.

18. C. Cardon, 'Two omphalos phialai', *GettyMJ* 6/7 (1978–79), 131–8 for clay examples.

19. The arguments for the theory can best be followed in M. J. Vickers, 'Artful crafts: the influence of metalwork on Athenian painted pottery', *JHS* 105 (1985), 102–28, pls. 4–6; M. J. Vickers (ed.), *Pots and Pans, a Colloquium on Precious Metals and Ceramics* (Oxford Series in Islamic Art, 3, Oxford, 1986), pp. 9–30 (Gill), 137–51 (Vickers), 217–23 (Raby and Vickers); M. Vickers, O. Impey and J. Allen, *From Silver to Ceramic* (Oxford, 1986); D. W. J. Gill, 'Expressions of wealth: Greek art and society', *Antiquity* 62 (1988), 735–43. The theory is linked to the downdating of material (see p. 7).

20. The books and articles listed in the previous note contain references to plate; see also especially R. A. Higgins (ed.), *Thracian Treasures from Bulgaria* (London, 1976); C. M. Danov, *Antique Tombs in Bulgaria* (Sofia, 1980); *Gold der Thraker, Archäologische Schätze aus Bulgarien* (Mainz, 1980); A. Fol, B. Nikolov and R. F. Hoddinott, *The New Thracian Treasure from Rogozen, Bulgaria* (London, 1986); B. F. Cook (ed.), *The Rogozen Treasure, Papers of the Anglo-Bulgarian Conference 12 March 1987* (London, 1989); M. Andronikos, *Vergina* (Athens, 1984); M. I. Artamonov, *Treasures from Skythian Tombs in the Hermitage Museum, Leningrad* (London, 1969); 'From the Land of the Skythians', Special Issue of the *Metr. Mus. Art Bull.* 32 (1973–74); B. Piotrovsky, L. Galanina, N. Grach, *Skythian Art* (Oxford and Leningrad, 1987); D. W. J. Gill, 'Two new silver shapes from Semibratny (Seven Brothers Tumuli)', *BSA* 82 (1987), 47–53. The silver work is usually considered to be Attic.

21. Tombs and metal, see nn. 19–20 above, and H. Hoffmann, 'Why did the Greeks need imagery? An anthropological approach to the study of Greek vase-painting', *Hephaistos* 9 (1988), 150–3, who considers most painted pottery was made primarily for the tomb or for dedication, not for domestic purposes.

22. B. B. Shefton, 'Persian gold and Attic black-glaze: Achaemenid influences on Attic pottery of the 5th and 4th centuries B.C.', *Annales archéologiques Arabes Syriennes* 21 (1971), 109–11, pls. 20–23, who accepts that some pottery has an effect on metalwork.

23. Ivory: M. J. Vickers, 'Les vases peints: image ou mirage', *Rouen Colloque*, pp. 29–42, figs. 1–7; 'The influence of exotic materials on Attic white-gound pottery', *Amsterdam Symposium*, pp. 88–97. Copper: M. Vickers, 'Silver, copper and ceramics in ancient Athens', *Pots and Pans* (n. 19, above), pp. 137–51.

24. K. Arafat and C. Morgan (n. 1, above), 336 'no such thing as bourgeois culture'; ideas ran from the top to the bottom of the social order.

25. See e.g. M. Robertson, 'Beazley and Attic Vase Painting', *Beazley and Oxford*, pp. 19–30; R. M. Cook, 'Artful crafts: a commentary', *JHS* 107 (1987), 169–71; J. Boardman, 'Silver is white', *RA* 1987, 279–95.

26. M. Robertson, *Beazley and Oxford*, p. 23.

VI. NARRATIVE AND IMAGES

Greek pottery provides us with a fascinating, if bewildering, variety of painted scenes. It is therefore no cause for astonishment that study of imagery, iconography, narrative method, mythical and contemporary subject matter,[1] etc. should be of major scholarly concern. Scholars work with the evidence they possess but have to keep in mind what is missing – both from literature and from art. The more closely investigated such matters are, the more obvious it becomes that we must be careful to make distinctions between the imagery of different centres of vase production,[2] and also between the imagery in vase-painting and that in other media, especially sculpture. It is inevitable that Athens has been the area most intensively probed, and that myth has been the most attractive magnet.

Myths

We approach Greek myths through sophisticated literary versions or through handbooks compiled by mythographers in later antiquity. Novel, intellectual ways of shaping myths were, however, for the few; for most Greeks, including vase-painters, there was no text of any sort, their grasp of a story was mainly oral.[3] Hence, any precedence that word may have had over image, must not be seen in terms of text versus picture; the stories were current in traditional versions before they were shaped by the poets. It is now generally agreed that the popularity of the earlier text-driven approach to the study of visual imagery was for the most part misguided, though not false in every instance. Emphasis now tends to be placed on the importance of vernacular, oral versions that circulated within families and local groups, with less stress given to the more formal, literary texts. Visual presentation, especially on pottery, is seen as a 'vulgar' version, not for the intelligentsia, rather for everyman. As Carpenter says, 'vase painters were neither theologians nor philosophers – not literary critics nor art historians . . . they were artisans who surely intended the imagery of their pictures (when they thought about it at all) to be accessible to the potential buyers',[4] and some of the modern esoteric interpretations of themes have been seen as demanding 'an improbable erudition for the craftsmen . . . and for their customers'.[5]

The measuring of myth in art by the extent to which it reflects a literary source is a limiting exercise. Vase-painters worked within their own graphic tradition and were more interested in conveying the essentials of a story than a particular version of it. The old task of using the incidence of myths in art for dating the Athenian 'edition' of Homer or for positing a missing epic (such as a supposed *Theseis* in the late sixth century) has less attractions amongst scholars today than previously, but is not entirely dead. The appearance and disappearance of certain myths, the particular episodes chosen, changes to the old traditional stories, all these variations are to be laid at the door of different causes: oral traditions and poetic innovations, iconographic conservativism, aesthetic considerations, cultic demands and preferences, family mythologizing, politics and history, and simple error. Time, place, function create changes in presentation.[6]

Modern approaches to the mythological stories depicted on pottery are wide-ranging. There has been a large output of volumes devoted to the illustrations of Greek myth, and the taxonomy is in full flow in *Lexicon Iconographicum Mythologiae Graecae* which is charting the visual images of characters and stories and has already become a basic work of reference.[7] Brommer's lists are also useful, despite their lack of illustrations and a rather idiosyncratic system of reference.[8] Schefold's volumes are picture books without compare, magisterially ordering the divine stories and heroic legends.[9] His view of Greek mythological imagery, though not to everyone's taste with its classification into chronological categories such as epic, dramatic, lyric, is a deeply felt personal vision of the religious foundations of Greek art. More manageable, if rather racy, is Henle's one-volume introduction.[10]

Many of the major stories, divine and heroic, have received detailed treatment, not confined to vase-paintings alone. The births and loves of the divinities raise interesting issues: why are goddesses born fully grown (e.g. Athena, Aphrodite) whereas gods start life as little babies?[11] And does the interest in the pursuits of deities after mortals in the late sixth and fifth centuries echo human aspirations or is it to be seen as consciousness of the gods' more specific participation in human affairs in the wake of such events as the expulsion of the tyrants from Athens and the repulse of the Persians from Greece?[12] The pursuit of Oreithyia by Boreas and of the nymph Aigina by Poseidon can both be seen in particular terms, the former in reference to the battle of Artemision, the latter the take-over of the island of Aigina by the Athenians.[13]

The story of the Argonauts is one for which early literary versions are sadly lacking, and it is inevitable that pictorial illustrations should be used to try and reach some idea of the thread of the story in the archaic and classical periods.[14] Considering the importance of the figures of Medea and Alkestis in literature, the pre-Euripidean versions have more than once been studied. The alterations the stories underwent make them excellent examples of the ways in which myths were constantly being transformed: Medea changes from fairy godmother into wicked witch, and Alkestis emerges from the group of murderous daughters of Pelias.[15] Moret used the Oedipus story with its early visual emphasis on the Sphinx as an object lesson in the distinctiveness of art and literature.[16] Few artists were interested in the tragic story of Oedipus himself. For Herakles and Theseus, see below.

The whole saga of Troy, from the Judgement of Paris to the returns of Agamemnon and Odysseus, is a quarry for study and raises problems of how to approach the subject – in the historical order of the episodes or in the chronological ordering of their making.[17] A fruitful essay has looked at the way in which one painter, the Kleophrades Painter, was attracted to themes from the Trojan cycle (Fig. 24).[18]

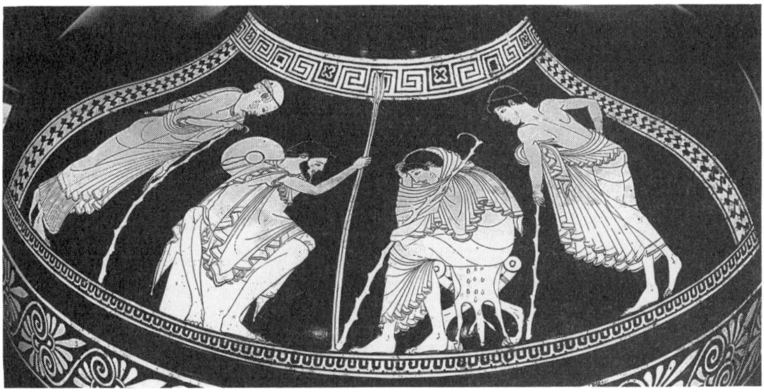

24. The embassy to Achilles. Attic red-figure hydria, attributed to the Kleophrades Painter. Ca. 480 B.C.

The beginnings of narrative

Two major concerns that have interested students have been the beginnings of narrative in the eighth century and the early methods of presenting a story, and the extent to which politics (particularly in Athens again) may have dictated themes and treatments in the sixth and fifth centuries.

The big narrative pictures on Late Geometric vases (Fig. 25) are some of the most impressive of any in the whole history of the craft.[19] The funerals, the lying-in-state and the transfer to the cemetery, the processions, the land- and sea-battles – how are we to understand

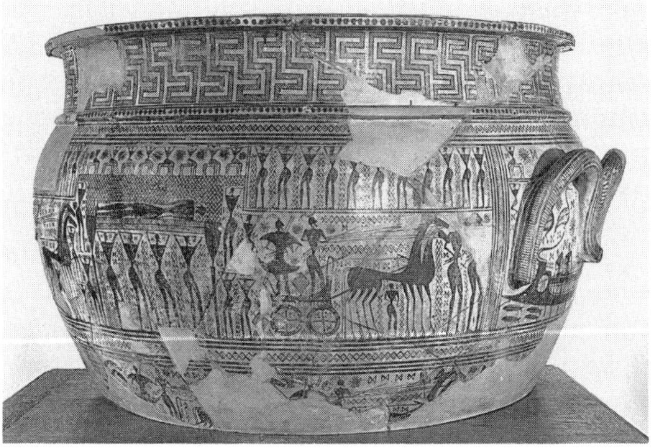

25. Attic Late Geometric krater with funeral scene. Ca. 750 B.C.

them? Are they contemporary scenes, symbolic and unparticular? Or are they heroic? And if so, in what way – specifically so, even though we cannot put names to the figures, or more generalized? The Homeric epics are now thought by some to be an unnecessarily confusing element, and the link between them and the rise of heroic imagery is considered false.[20] As propositions worthy of discussion, we have '1. that Homer probably never saw an Attic Geometric vase in his life and that the only sophisticated figure art he knew was probably foreign (this is not the moment to discuss his blindness); 2. that no Attic Geometric artist had ever read or heard recited a single line of Homer.'[21]

The specificity of the narrative once established, we then face the problem of the method in which it was represented, particularly if it was a narrative with various stages or episodes. The desire of the painter to present an intelligible scene leads him to include elements and moments that are not contemporary. Students of narrative techniques propose four methods:[22] the monoscenic (the essential, dramatic moment, the 'photographic shot'); the synoptic (successive episodes in one vision – an essentially non-literary procedure, e.g. Fig. 26); the cyclic (the repetition of a figure in different episodes, e.g. Theseus in metopes and on some Attic red-figure cups); and the continuous (a system of presentation without divisions which we find most clearly in Roman art, e.g. best known from Trajan's column). It is the synoptic which is considered to be widespread and frequent in the Archaic period – not as a sophisticated refinement of an earlier monoscenic treatment but rather as a naive or natural answer to the demands laid upon an artist when illustrating a narrative.

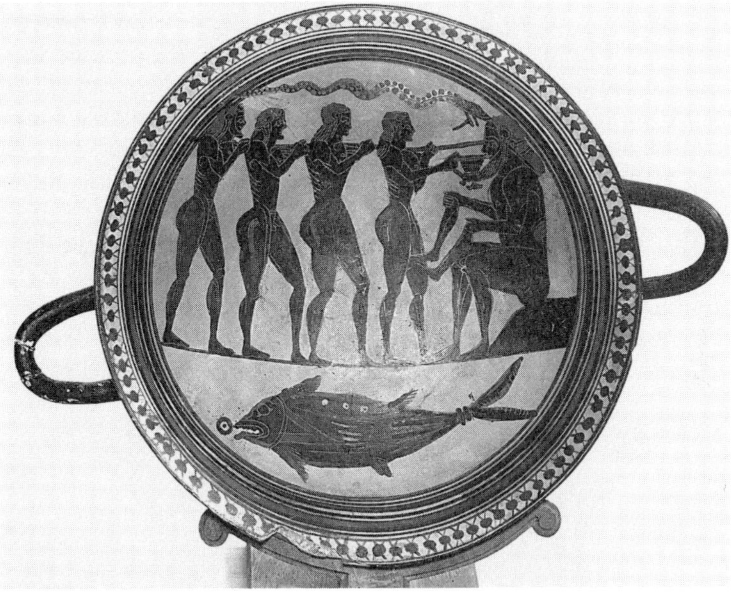

26. The blinding of the Cyclops. Laconian black-figure cup. Ca. 540 B.C.

The question of the source of any story in art and the reason for its being used at one time rather than another, is still a battlefield. Literary sources have their proponents, but greater care has to be taken over the ground rules. Robert Cook has spelled them out in his usual trenchant way, specifically in relation to art and epic (the six Trojan ones, in particular) in the Archaic period.[23] The possible reasons for a subject being found both in art and in epic are listed as: coincidence; a poet borrowing from an artist; an artist borrowing from a poet; both taking from a common source. If borrowing by artist from poet is to be accepted, it must meet the requirements of either a detail invented by the poet, or several episodes from the same epic appearing in art at the same time, or a range of episodes which occur in one epic. His conclusion is 'though there is no proof either way, the probabilities are that in the period covered – that is down to about 530 B.C. – Greek artists did not regularly or often make deliberate use of epic poetry for their subjects, but preferred the folktales they knew, probably from childhood.'

If we may leave epic and look at lyric, Stesichoros (fl. 570–540 B.C.) is an author whose work has been thought to have an influence on the work of vase-painters. Publication of the papyrus text of his *Geryoneis* gave rise to Martin Robertson's study of possible artistic connections, and more recently Brize has looked more closely at links between the poet and art.[24] The difficulties of establishing such a connection must not be minimized, especially in view of the author's western origins. There were ancient claims that Stesichoros was responsible for certain literary innovations (Herakles' club, lion skin, and bow, and Athena appearing fully armed from the head of Zeus), but these have been shown to be ill founded, and the association that Stewart felt he had detected between Stesichoros' work and the François vase has been thought tenuous.[25]

Drama has been shown to have had a specific and a general effect.[26] Tragic insights, whether based on individual tragedies or not, are reflected in the scenes of divine punishment (e.g. the Niobids), and the

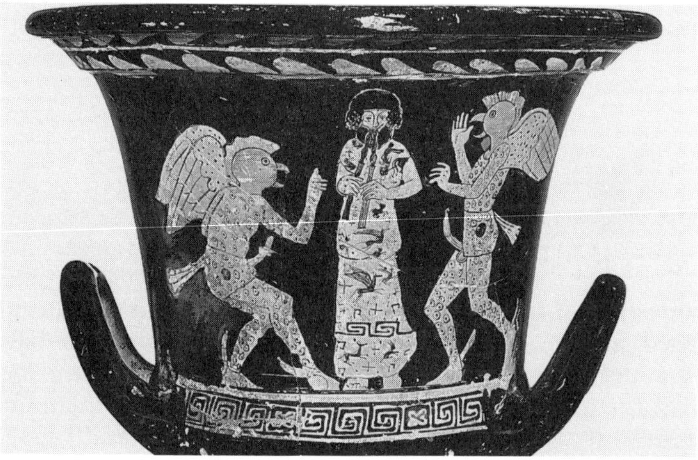

27. Comic scene with birds and pipeplayer. Attic (?) red-figure calyx-krater. Late fifth century B.C.

concentration on the dramatic or heightened moment may be attributed to the influence of the new literary form. Attic artists rarely used themes that are found in tragedy, whereas for the vase-painters of South Italy and Sicily they are an important element.[27] Satyr plays can be reflected in vase-paintings,[28] and on occasion comedy finds itself represented.[29] The birds in comic costume (Fig. 27) have been seen as derived from Aristophanes' *Birds* or from the original (lost) version of his *Clouds* in which we are told two fighting cocks were brought on stage in cages. A play of Menander has recently been recognized on a Centuripe pyxis.[30]

A healthy refusal to be too strongly constrained by texts has led to a widening appreciation of the influences at work on the painters. 'No one poet or poem dominated the treatment in art of any single cycle of stories and, unless we are still lacking all information about some source or poet, more influential than we can imagine, we must judge the artist's view of any story to be conditioned by many different sources, not least his own memory, which may be defective, as well as the traditions and conventions of his art, and, of course, the appeal of his own imagination and emotions.'[31]

Politics

The widening search for the sources that inspired subjects on vases has embraced the world of politics, and as if to compensate for the reduction in connection between vase-paintings and literary texts, political allusions on vases have been seized on with eagerness. Herakles – Superman, saviour of mankind – is the most popular hero in Greek myth, and Frank Brommer has collected and ordered the episodes in his career in all media.[32] Indeed, the concentration that has recently been directed at his political usefulness, should not blind us to the much larger importance of his total significance.[33] Brommer himself has tended to steer clear of any involvement with the possible political origins of the iconographical changes in Herakles' exploits. However, it is the political aspect that has recently led the field, and John Boardman, who began the recent chase, has pursued his quarry with more care and persistence than some of his less cautious followers.[34] The major connection suggested has been that between Herakles and Peisistratos in sixth-century Athenian vase-painting – what Boardman has called 'the Herakles phenomenon'. Most recently, he has defended his thesis of 'political manipulation of myth' in art against attack.[35] Myths were always being used as a reflector and, like all mirrors, could be made to present distorted images. Boardman's main points are that Herakles was traditionally considered the protégé of Athena, Athens' goddess; that he was overwhelmingly present in the art and architectural sculpture of archaic Athens, though rarely before the sixth century and less so subsequently; that he was less popular at that time in other parts of Greece; that there were new themes introduced then; and that Athens was the first to worship him as a god. As for his equation with Peisistratos, he finds this only natural 'given his special relationship with the goddess', and he sees that his popularity in art 'gives the hero a special role in Athenian life and politics, rather than cult'. The manipulation of the myths was not in the hands of vase-painters, who merely reflect new opinions and stories; the vases were 'not the medium for any deliberate political propaganda'.

Boardman was specifically answering a cautionary note sounded by Robert Cook who had felt that 'arguments for the politically allusive and still more for the propagandist theory are too tenuous to be convincing'.[36] Cook wished to distinguish deliberate party propaganda from reflections of the results of political action, and concentrated on the former. He saw difficulties in the equation of a living person with a god or hero, with the actual means by which political propaganda was devised and adopted (an emissary of Peisistratos' court popping down to the Kerameikos to order a Herakles special?). He found against the major themes that have been thought to refer to Peisistratos: 'Herakles harnessing a chariot, for his journey to Olympus with Athena' (Fig. 28) being equated with Peisistratos' return to Athens accompanied by Phye of Paeania dressed as Athena (Herodotos 1.60); 'Herakles versus Triton' as a reference to Peisistratos'

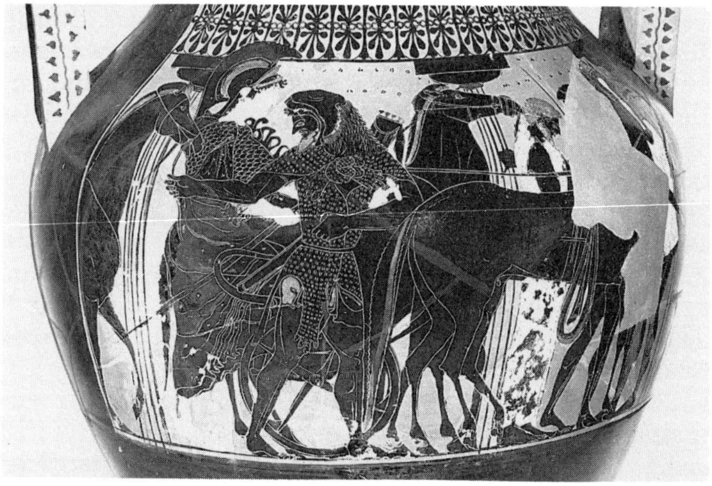

28. Herakles and Athena. Attic black-figure amphora, attributed to the Priam Painter. Late sixth century B.C.

campaign against Megara in 566 B.C. (1.59); 'Ajax and Achilles dicing' alluding to the battle at Pallene and Peisistratos' victory over his dicing or sleeping opponents (1.63). However, Boardman and Cook are both united in stressing that all these connections are probabilities; it is the degree to which these probabilities are judged likely, that separates them.

Theseus is the other major figure who has been seen as a 'political' hero; his cycle of stories, from Troizen to Athens, was invented in the late sixth century to establish him as an important 'home-grown' Athenian figure.[37] He is usually seen as a post-Kleisthenic hero who represents the newly established democracy.[38] His most popular period comes after the Persian Wars, when the search for Theseus' bones was successfully concluded by Kimon on the island of Skyros, and a sanctuary was built for the hero in the centre of Athens. Indeed, Theseus is seen as a particularly Kimonian 'protégé'.[39] The changing fortunes of Herakles and Theseus have been seen to be exemplified in the Amazonomachies. What had in the sixth century been an expedition to Themiskyra by Herakles becomes a joint campaign for Herakles and Theseus, but later the emphasis and the locale change, and it is Theseus who is shown throwing back the invading Amazons from Athens itself. Are we to see Theseus' involvement at Themiskyra as a reference to Athenian aid given to Ephesos at the time of the Ionian revolt of 499 B.C., and his fighting in Athens an allusion to the Athenians' successful repulse of the invading Persians from the soil of Attica twenty years later?[40] Victory in all these sorts of academic skirmish goes to those who manage to give rein to their ingenuity whilst retaining a grasp of reality.

Structuralism

The study of Greek myth has undergone a considerable change in the last twenty years,[41] and the new directions have affected the approaches to the visual arts no less than to other types of evidence. So, the more traditional lines of enquiry into the subject matter of Greek art are now being pursued alongside investigations that are concerned with such matters as perception theory and semiotics.

Iconography has been a popular and productive subject for study, and the continuing *Lexicon Iconographicum Mythologiae Graecae*[42] is now carrying it out on a grand scale for the divine and heroic myths and personalities. The study involves tracing repeated images and taking note of the appearance of new subjects and uncanonical treatments. Myth is treated as myth, and the development of each story, in time and place, with its episodes and variants, and with its rise and fall in popularity, is painstakingly charted. The whole approach is intellectual and rational, using literature as a guideline to which the visual images adhere or from which they depart. But even such a committed student of iconography as Brommer has to admit that 'to approach myth by way of reason is like measuring color differences with a ruler.'[43]

Here is where new approaches make their entrance, and for some the term 'iconography' gives way to 'iconology'.[44] The angle of reference is broadened; myths are not treated solely nor even primarily as myths – it is not the surface appearance that is studied, it is the underlying structure expressed in symbolic terms that has to be unearthed. It is not only myth that lends itself to this type of investigation, scenes of everyday life are susceptible to analysis; indeed the dichotomy between myth and genre is felt to be false, or at least unimportant.[45] What the structuralists are trying to reveal are the unconscious, subliminal forces at work that break out in the form of images that need to be decoded – 'the recovery of the implicit categories – the structures – in terms of which "Greek mentality" is articulated'.[46] This structuralist approach is essentially unhistorical. As Snodgrass has expressed their viewpoint, 'a given myth is made up of all its variants, . . . the narrative sequence and content of all or any of these variants is unimportant and . . . what matters is the structure of the myth, reflecting as it does the structure of the human mind'.[47] So much for our punctilious concern with details and variants! The two approaches – the iconographical and the iconological – are sharply opposed, the former accords with the classicist's credo, the latter takes us amongst the anthropologists and is concerned with the 'relationship between social practices and institutions, on the one hand, and their ideological counterparts in myth and literature, on the other'.[48]

Let us look at a few examples of the ways in which the structuralist approach has been applied. Although such study can be directed towards any figured scene, no matter where produced, once again most work has been carried out on the rich evidence that the Attic vase-painters have left.

(a) Animals have been seen to represent a 'complex taxonomic system'. They are not to be thought of simply as attributes of divinities or as mere ornament. The game-cock has been studied in some depth to show the different symbolic meanings that it personifies: martial courage in the fight reflects the courage of the hero, but when held by cupids, the birds take on an erotic symbolism that the many scenes of courting youths and men reveal more openly. But the cock is also to be seen in a funerary context, e.g. on white-ground lekythoi.[49]

(b) Animals are also involved in scenes of hunt and of sacrifice, and these have been studied for the information they can give us of Greek society and its attitudes to the boundaries between wild nature and civilization. Here it can be readily seen that the myth of Meleager and the boar can be studied alongside images of everyday hunting scenes and treated to the same sort of structural analysis.[50]

(c) Erotic pursuits, including those to which mythological names are attached, have been shown to have layers of meaning that relate them to rites of passage, whether sexual or funerary. An armed youth pursuing a woman (e.g. Fig. 29) is a 'polyvalent' image and has to be considered in relation to all other such images.[51] As examples of the

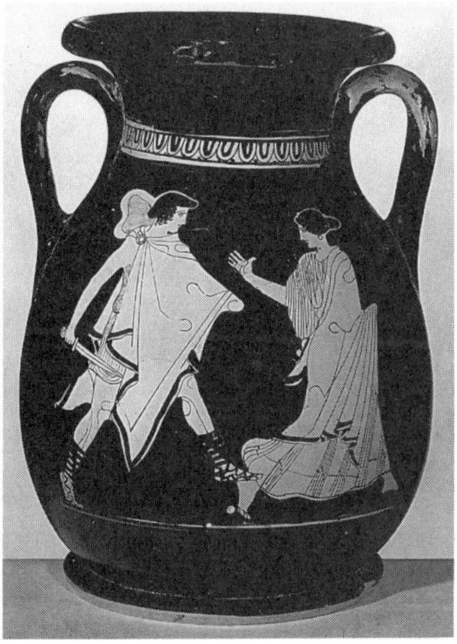

29. Armed youth pursues a woman (Theseus attacking Medea?). Attic red-figure pelike. Ca. 440–430 B.C.

funerary aspect of pursuit, one might instance the two stamnoi from the Brygos Tomb (Colour Plate 4A) which show Eos, the goddess of Dawn, abducting the young man Kephalos, a theme that has associations with death before one's time.

(d) The scenes of symposium, which are one of the mainstays of Attic cup decoration, have been seen as having a ritual significance, as they are linked with Dionysos who possesses you when you take him into yourself. Thus the banquet scenes have intimations of immortality about them. Dionysian imagery is rich and full, and perhaps lends itself too easily to structuralist decoding.[52]

(e) The fights and loves of the Amazons were popular themes in art, and, as well as being capable of historical interpretation in particular ways, have also been seen as indicators of social attitudes.[53]

(f) The images of Artemis have been studied for what they reveal about the Greeks' complex religious beliefs. The important finds of painted pottery and sculptured reliefs from the sanctuary of Artemis at Brauron on the east coast of Attica show contrasts in the imagery of the goddess: virginity and procreation; wild nature and civic order; initiation to married life and ritual death.[54]

For some scholars, the structuralist approaches to the scenes on Greek painted pottery are jejune. 'Structuralism . . . seems to be a dying creed because Greek myth is too sophisticated to demonstrate convincingly its simplistic method, and because it abjures the historic approach that is basic to our studies.'[55] For others, it is a new and exciting way forward that may help students of Greek art come to a fuller understanding of the mainsprings of the complex world of Greek imagery. Whatever one's stance, these new approaches are making scholars think hard about the different meanings of the images, their contexts, and the functions they were intended to perform.

NOTES

1. For some of the areas of Greek life that vase-paintings are used to illuminate, see on festivals: H. W. Parke, *Festivals of the Athenians* (London, 1977), E. Simon, *Festivals of Attica:*

an archaeological commentary (University of Wisconsin Press, 1983), A. W. Pickard-Cambridge, *The Dramatic Festivals of Athens*, 2nd edition revised with supplements and corrections by J. Gould and D. M. Lewis (Oxford, 1988); for symposia: G. Hagenau, *Aus dem Weingarten der Antike* (Mainz, 1982), F. Lissarrague, *Un flot d'images – une esthétique du banquet grec* (Paris, 1987), O Murray (ed.), *Sympotica, a symposium on the Symposion* (Oxford, 1990); for sex: J. Boardman and E. La Rocca, *Eros in Greece* (London, 1978), K. J. Dover, *Greek Homosexuality* (London, 1978), C. Johns, *Sex or Symbol: erotic images of Greece and Rome* (London, 1982); for death: D. C. Kurtz and J. Boardman, *Greek Burial Customs* (London, 1971), E. Vermeule, *Aspects of Death in Early Greek Art and Poetry* (University of California Press, 1979), R. Garland, *The Greek Way of Death* (London, 1985). See later for such aspects as the hunt, sacrifice, etc.

2. See e.g. M. Pipili's recent study, *Laconian Iconography of the Sixth Century B.C.* (Oxford University Committee for Archaeology, monograph 12, 1987).

3. E. A. Havelock, *Prologue to Greek Literacy* (Cincinnati, 1971), *The Literate Revolution in Greece and its Cultural Consequences* (Princeton, 1982), *The Muse Learns to Write* (Yale UP, 1986); B. Gentili, *Poetry and its Public in Ancient Greece* (Baltimore, 1988); W. V. Harris, *Ancient Literacy* (Harvard, 1989).

4. T. H. Carpenter, *Dionysian Imagery in Archaic Greek Art* (Oxford, 1986), xvi.

5. R. M. Cook, *Clazomenian Sarcophagi* (see IV, n. 14), 130.

6. See A. H. Shapiro, *Art and Cult under the Tyrants in Athens* (Mainz, 1989) and E. D. Francis, *Image and Idea in Fifth-century Greece* (London, 1990).

7. *Lexicon Iconographicum Mythologiae Graecae*, ed. L. Kahil (Zurich and Munich, 1981–).

8. F. Brommer, *Denkmälerlisten zur griechischen Heldensage* 1–4 (Marburg, 1971–76) – not vases; *Vasenlisten zur griechischen Heldensage*, 3rd ed. (Marburg, 1973); *Göttersagen in Vasenlisten* (Marburg, 1980).

9. K. Schefold, *Myth and Legend in Early Greek Art* (London, 1966); *Götter- und Heldensagen der Griechen in der spätarchaischen Kunst* (Munich, 1978); *Die Göttersage in der klassischen und hellenistischen Kunst* (Munich, 1981); (with F. Jung) *Die Urkönige, Perseus, Bellerophon, Herakles und Theseus in der klassischen und hellenistischen Kunst* (Munich, 1988); a final volume to come on the group enterprises.

10. J. Henle, *Greek Myths: a vase-painter's notebook* (Bloomington, 1973), with useful bibliography; for another bibliography, see Moon *AGAI*, pp. 301–32. A volume by T. H. Carpenter, *Art and Myth in Ancient Greece*, has now appeared (1991).

11. E. H. Loeb, *Die Geburt der Götter in der griechischen Kunst der klassischer Zeit* (Jerusalem, 1979). See S. Woodford's review in *JHS* 101 (1981), 221–2. See also K. Arafat, *Classical Zeus* (Oxford, 1990), chs. 2 & 3.

12. S. Kaempf-Dimitriadou, *Die Liebe der Götter in der attischen Kunst des 5. Jahrhunderts v. Chr.* (*AK* Beiheft 11, Bern, 1979).

13. Boreas: E. Simon 'Boreas und Oreithyia auf dem silbernen Rhyton in Triest', *Antike und Abenland* 13 (1967), 101–27, figs. 1–20 and colour plate, esp. 111–17. Aegina: *LIMC* I. 367–71 (S. Kaempf. Dimitriadou); K. Arafat, *Classical Zeus* (Oxford, 1990), pp. 77-88.

14. M. Vojatzi, *Frühe Argonautenbilder* (Würzburg, 1982).

15. H. Meyer, *Medeia und die Peliaden: eine attische Novelle und ihre Entstehung. Ein Versuch zur Sagenforschung auf archäologischer Grundlage* (Rome, 1980) and see IV, n. 41 (Ohly-Dumm). See also C. Sourvinou-Inwood, *Theseus as Son and Stepson* (*BICS* Suppl. 40, 1979).

16. J.-M. Moret, *Oedipe, la sphinx et les Thébains: essai de mythologie iconographique* (Geneva, 1984).

17. The bibliography on the Trojan saga and its aftermath is long. For some various approaches, see J.-M. Moret, 'Le jugement de Pâris en Grande-Grèce: mythe et actualité politique', *AK* 21 (1978), 76–98, pls. 21–8. For Peleus and Thetis, see IV, n. 25 (Williams) and n. 26 (Stewart), and n. 3, above, ch. 1. For other themes, see M. I. Davies, 'The Reclamation of Helen', *AK* 20 (1977), 73–85, pl. 17; W. Batista, 'Hektors Lösung', *Boreas* 2 (1979), 5–36; D. Williams, 'Ajax, Odysseus and the arms of Achilles', *AK* 23 (1980), 137–45, pls. 33–6; M. I. Davies, 'Ajax at the bourne of life', *ΕΙΔΩΛΟΠΟΙΙΑ, Actes du colloque sur les problèmes de l'image dans la monde méditerranéen classique, Château de Lourmarin en Provence 2–3 Septembre 1982*, ed. H. Metzger (Rome, 1985), pp. 82–117, pls. 1–2; J.-M. Moret, *L'Ilioupersis dans la*

céramique italiote (Geneva, 1975); A. J. N. W. Prag, *The Oresteia: Iconographic and Narrative Tradition* (Warminster, 1985); F. Brommer, *Odysseus. Die Taten und Leiden des Helden in antiker Kunst, und Literatur* (Darmstadt, 1983); *The Quest for Ulysses*, edd. W. B. Stanford and J. V. Luce (London, 1974); B. Rubens and O. Taplin, *An Odyssey round Odysseus* (London, 1989).

18. J. Boardman, 'The Kleophrades Painter at Troy', *AK* 19 (1976), 3–18, pls. 1–3.

19. G. Ahlberg, *Prothesis and Ekphora in Greek Geometric Art* (Göteborg, 1971); *Fighting on Land and Sea in Greek Geometric Art* (Stockholm, 1971). See also T. Rombos, *The Iconography of Attic Late Geometric II Pottery* (Jonsered, 1988).

20. K. Fittschen, *Untersuchungen zum Beginn der Sagendarstellungen bei den Griechen* (Berlin, 1969) is a full treatment. A. M. Snodgrass has looked at the problem from time to time: 'Poet and painter in eighth century Greece', *PCPS* 205 (1979), 118–30; 'Towards an interpretation of the Geometric figure-scenes', *AM* 95 (1980), 51–8, pls. 11–14; *Archaic Greece, the age of experiment* (London, 1980), 65–77; 'La naissance du récit dans l'art grec', *Lausanne Colloque*, pp. 11–18; 'The first figure-scenes in Greek art', *An Archaeology of Greece* (University of California Press, 1987), ch. 5. See also J. Carter, 'The beginnings of narrative art in the Greek Geometric period', *BSA* 67 (1972), 25–58, pls. 5–12.

21. J. Boardman, 'Symbol and story in Geometric art', Moon *AGAI*, pp. 15–36 (quotation from p. 29); another view, J. L. Benson, 'Symptom and story in Geometric art', *BABesch* 63 (1988), 69–76. See also R. Kannicht, 'Poetry and Art. Homer and the monuments afresh', *Classical Antiquity* 1 (1982), 70–86, pls. 1–6.

22. See J. M. Hemelrijk, *Gnomon* 42 (1970), 166–71; A. M. Snodgrass, *Narration and Allusion in Archaic Greek Art* (London, 1982) and *An Archaeology of Greece* (University of California Press, 1987), ch. 5. See also M. Davies, 'A convention of metamorphosis in Greek art', *JHS* 106 (1986), 182–3, pl. 8, and H. Froning, 'Anfänge der kontinuirenden Bilderzählung in der griechischer Kunst', *JDAI* 103 (1988), 169–99.

23. R. M. Cook, 'Art and epic in Archaic Greece', *BABesch* 58 (1983), 1–10 (quotation from 6). H. A. Shapiro, 'Herakles and Kyknos', *AJA* 88 (1984), 323–9, pls. 68–9, has made a good case for thc Herakles and Kyknos illustrations being based on the version in the pseudo-Hesiodic *Shield of Herakles*.

24. M. Robertson, 'Geryoneis: Stesichorus and the vase-painters', *CQ* 19 (1969), 207–21; P. Brize, *Die Geryoneis des Stesichoros und die frühe griechische Kunst* (Würzburg, 1980); 'Samos und Stesichoros. Zu einem früharchaischen Bronzeblech', *AM* 100 (1985), 54–90, pls. 15–24 and Beil. 2.

25. See n. 18, above, 11–13 and IV, n. 26.

26. A. D. Trendall and T. B. L. Webster, *Illustrations of Greek Drama* (London, 1971) gives a selection of Attic and South Italian theatrical scenes. See also J. R. March, *The Creative Poet* (BICS Supplement 49, 1987). For dithyrambs and vases, see H. Froning, *Dithyrambos und Vasenmalerei in Athen* (Würzburg, 1971) and J. H. Oakley, 'A calyx-krater in Virginia by the Nikias Painter with the birth of Erichthonios', *AK* 39 (1987), 123–30, pls. 18–19.

27. See e.g. A. Kossatz-Deissmann, *Dramen des Aischylos auf westgriechischen Vasen* (Mainz, 1978).

28. E. Simon, 'Satyr-plays on vases from the time of Aeschylus', *Eye of Greece*, pp. 123–48, pls. 30–40; L. Burn, 'A heron on the left, by the Kodros Painter', *Copenhagen Symposium*, pp. 99–105. See also, for a wider view, F. Lissarrague, 'Why satyrs are good to represent', *Nothing to do with Dionysus*, edd. J. J. Winkler and F. I. Zeitlin (Princeton, 1989), pp. 228–36, pls. 1–16.

29. J. R. Green, 'A representation of the Birds of Aristophanes', *Greek Vases* II (1985), 95–118; O.Taplin, 'Phallology, *Phlyakes*, Iconography and Aristophanes', *PCPS* 213 (1987), 92–104 (he also discusses the South Italian Telephos bell-krater (*Thesm.* 96–99), first published by A. Kossats-Deissman, 'Telephus transvestitus', *Tainia*, pp. 281–90, pls. 60–61, and now illustrated in E. Simon, *The Ancient Theatre*, trans. C. E. Vaphopoulou-Richardson (London, 1982), pl. 15).

30. E. Simon, *Menander in Centuripe* (Stuttgart, 1989), with full references to other Meander representations.

31. Quotation from n. 16 above, p. 11. See also H. Metzger, 'Beazley et l'image', *AK* 30 (1987), 109–18, pls. 15–16, on Beazley's adherence to the literary text in interpretating a scene.

32. F. Brommer, *Herakles. Die zwölf Taten des Helden in antiken Kunst und Literatur*, 4th

ed. (Darmstadt, 1979), translated and enlarged by S. J. Schwarz as *Herakles. The Twelve Labors of the Hero in Ancient Art and Literature* (New York, 1980), and *Herakles II. Die unkanonischen Taten des Helden* (Darmstadt, 1984). See also *Denkmälerlisten zur griechischen Heldensage* I (Marburg, 1971) and *Vasenlisten zur griechischen Heldensage*, 3rd ed. (Marburg, 1973), pp. 1–209.

33. See G. K. Galinsky, *The Herakles Theme* (Oxford, 1972) and R. Vollkommer, *Herakles in the Art of Classical Greece* (Oxford University Committee for Archaeology, monograph 25, 1988).

34. The literature is now extensive. See particularly J. Boardman's contributions: 'Herakles, Peisistratos and sons', *RA* 1972, 57–72; 'Herakles, Peisistratos and Eleusis', *JHS* 95 (1975), 1–12, pls. 1–4; 'Herakles, Delphi and Kleisthenes of Sikyon', *RA* 1978, 227–34; 'Exekias', *AJA* 82 (1978), 18–24; 'Image and politics in sixth century Athens', *Amsterdam Symposium*, pp. 239–47.

35. 'Herakles, Peisistratos and the unconvinced', *JHS* 109 (1989), 158–9. 'That Greeks used their myth-history as a mirror to their life, and one which they could readily distort to suit their needs and circumstances, is a commonplace' (159).

36. 'Pots and Peisistratan Propaganda', *JHS* 107 (1987), 167–9. This note contains references to many extensions and counterarguments to Boardman's ideas. One might single out R. Osborne's 'The myth of propaganda and the propaganda of myth', *Hephaistos* 5/6 (1983/4), 61–70, pls. 1–2, and an overingenious attempt to relate 'Herakles versus Nereus' to Solon's struggle against civil unrest, G. Ahlberg-Cornell, *Herakles and the Sea-Monster in Attic Black-Figure Vase-painting* (Stockholm, 1984). For a general comment on political symbolism, see Arafat and Morgan (V, n. 1), 231–4.

37. F. Brommer, *Theseus. Die Taten des griechischen Helden in der antiken Kunst und Literatur* (Darmstadt, 1982). See also *Denkmälerlisten zur griechischen Heldensage* II (Marburg, 1971), pp. 1–28 and *Vasenlisten zur griechischen Heldensage*, 3rd ed. (Marburg, 1973), pp. 210–58. For a popular treatment, see *The Quest for Theseus*, ed. A. G. Ward (London, 1970). See also J. Neils, *The Youthful Deeds of Theseus* (Rome, 1987). See also E. D. Francis (n. 6 above).

38. See C. Sourvinou-Inwood, 'Theseus lifting the rock and a cup near the Pithos Painter', *JHS* 91 (1971), 94–109, pl. 12.

39. See J. P. Barron, 'New light on old walls: the murals of the Theseion', *JHS* 92 (1972), 20–45, pls. 1–7; 'Bakchylides, Theseus and a woolly cloak', *BICS* 27 (1980), 1–8. For a stress on the earlier importance of Theseus, see H. A. Shapiro, 'Theseus and the creation of an Athenian national hero', *AJA* 93 (1989), 279. For Kimonian influence on Polygnotos' panel paintings, see R. B. Kebric, *The Paintings in the Cnidian Lesche at Delphi and the Historical Context* (Leiden, 1983). Kebric sees Eurymedon as the catalyst for the Cnidians' dedication, but for another, more scabrous way of expressing Eurymedon, see the Attic red-figure oinochoe in Hamburg, K. Schauenburg, '*ΕΥΡΥΜΕΔΩΝ ΕΙΜΙ*', *AM* 90 (1975), 197–121, pl. 15 and for a different interpretation, G. F. Pinney, 'For the heroes are at hand', *JHS* 104 (1984), 181–3, pl. 8 c–d.

40. J. Boardman, 'Herakles, Theseus and Amazons', *Eye of Greece*, p. 1–28, pls. 1–6. See also Gauer (see III, n. 28).

41. E.g. W. Burkert, *Structure and History in Greek Mythyology and Ritual* (University of California Press, 1979); R. L. Gordon (ed.), *Myth, Religion and Society* (Cambridge and Paris, 1981); J. Bremmer (ed.), *Interpretations of Greek Mythology* (London and Sydney, 1987); L. Edmunds (ed.), *Approaches to Greek Myth* (Baltimore and London, 1990).

42. See n. 7, above.

43. F. Brommer, *Herakles. The Twelve Labors* (see n. 32, above), p. 2.

44. The most entertaining introduction to this subject is C. Bérard and others, *La Cité des Images, Religion et Société en Grèce antique* (Fernard Nathan – L.E.P., 1984), now *A City of Images, Iconography and Society in Ancient Greece*, trans. D. Lyons (Princeton, 1989). Subjects considered are the warrior, sacrifice and the hunt, Eros as hunter, women, festivals and mysteries, wine, satyrs, and masks.

45. The French/Swiss have been some of the foremost proponents of the new approaches; of those concerning themselves with art, one might mention C. Bérard, F. Lissarrague, J.-L. Durand and A. Schnapp. There have been many recent conferences (Rouen, Provence, Paris) that have been devoted to the subject of myth and its interpretation. Of those scholars writing in English, one might single out a German, Herbert Hoffmann: *Sexual and Asexual*

Pursuit. A structuralist approach to Greek vase-painting (RAI, Occasional Paper 34, London, 1977); 'In the wake of Beazley', *Hephaistos* 1 (1979), 61–70; 'Iconography and Iconology', *Hephaistos* 7–8 (1985–6), 61–66; 'The cicada on the omphalos: an iconographical excursion', *Antiquity* 62 (1988), 744–9; 'Why did the Greeks need imagery? An anthropological approach to the study of Greek vase-painting', *Hephaistos* 9 (1988), 143–62 (cf. A. Schnapp, Why did the Greeks need images?', *Copenhagen Symposium*, pp. 568–74).

46. R. L. Gordon (ed.), *Myth, Religion and Society* (see n. 41, above), ix (Buxton).

47. A. M. Snodgrass, *An Archaeology of Greece* (California, 1987), p. 135.

48. R. L. Gordon (ed.), *Myth, Religion and Society* (see n. 41, above), xi (Buxton).

49. H. Hoffman, 'Hahnenkampf in Athen. Zur Ikonologie einer attischen Bildformel', *RA* 1974, 195–220; *Hephaistos* 9 (1988) (see n. 45, above).

50. A. Schnapp, 'Images et programme: les figurations archaïques de la chasse au sanglier', *RA* 1979, 195–218; F. Lissarrague and J.-L. Durand, 'Les entrailles de la cité', *Hephaistos* 1 (1979), 81–108, pls. 1–3; P. Schnitt and A. Schnapp, 'Image et société en Grèce ancienne: les représentations de la chasse et du banquet', *RA* 1982, 57–74; A. Schnapp, 'Héraclès, Thésée et les chasseurs: les ambiguités du héros', *Lausanne Colloque*, p. 121–30. See also n. 44, above. For the larger view, see W. Burkert, *Homo Necans. The Anthropology of Ancient Greek Sacrificial Ritual and Myth,* trans. P. Bing (California, 1983).

51. C. Sourvinou-Inwood, *Theseus as Son and Stepson* (*BICS* Suppl. 40, 1979); 'Menace and pursuit: differentiation and the creation of meaning', *Lausanne Colloque,* pp. 41–58; 'A series of erotic pursuits: images and meanings', *JHS* 107 (1987), 131–53, pl. 2b–3; 'Myths in Images: Theseus and Medea as a case study', L. Edmunds (ed.), *Approaches to Greek Myth* (see n. 41, above), pp. 393–445; C. Bérard, 'Le chassaresse traquée: cynégétique et érotique', *Kanon,* 280–4, pls. 83–4. See also n. 44, above.

52. See T. H. Carpenter, *Dionysian Imagery in archaic Greek art* (Oxford, 1986); F. Lissarrague, *Un flot d'images, une esthétique du banquet grec* (Paris, 1987); H. Hoffman, 'Rhyta and Kantharoi in Greek Ritual', *Greek Vases* IV (1989), 131–66. For satyrs, see n. 28, above.

53. W. B. Tyrrell, *Amazons, a study in Athenian mythmaking* (Baltimore and London, 1984); L. Hardwick, 'Ancient Amazons – heroes, outsiders or women?' *Greece & Rome* 37 (1990), 14–36.

54. L. Kahil, 'L'Artémis de Brauron: rites et mystère', *AK* 20 (1977), 86–98, pls. 18–21; 'La déesse Artémis: mythologie et iconographie', *Greece and Italy in the Classical World. Acta of the XI International Congress of Classical Archaeology* (London, 1979), pp. 73–87, pls. 31–6; 'Le "cratérisque" d'Artemis et le Brauronion de l'Acropole', *Hesperia* 50 (1981), 253–63, pl. 62; 'Mythological Repertoire of Brauron', Moon *AGAI*, pp. 231–44; C. Sourvinou-Inwood, *Studies in Girls' Transitions* (Athens, 1988); K. Dowden, *Dream and the Maiden. Girls' Initiation Rites in Greek Mythology* (London and New York, 1989).

55. J. Boardman, 'Image and Politics in Sixth Century Athens', *Amsterdam Symposium*, p. 241.